Leadership
LEGACY

Using Insights from Your Past to
Build a Legacy of Success

TRINETTE PIERRE

WESTBOW
PRESS®
A DIVISION OF THOMAS NELSON
& ZONDERVAN

WestBow Press books may be ordered through booksellers or by contacting:

WestBow Press
A Division of Thomas Nelson & Zondervan
1663 Liberty Drive
Bloomington, IN 47403
www.westbowpress.com
844-714-3454

Because of the dynamic nature of the Internet, any web addresses or links contained in this book may have changed since publication and may no longer be valid. The views expressed in this work are solely those of the author and do not necessarily reflect the views of the publisher, and the publisher hereby disclaims any responsibility for them.

Any people depicted in stock imagery provided by Getty Images are models, and such images are being used for illustrative purposes only. Certain stock imagery © Getty Images.

Scripture quotations marked (NLT) are taken from the Holy Bible, New Living Translation, copyright ©1996, 2004, 2015 by Tyndale House Foundation. Used by permission of Tyndale House Publishers, Carol Stream, Illinois 60188. All rights reserved. -Scripture marked (KJV) taken from the King James Version.

ISBN: 978-1-6642-8431-9 (sc)
ISBN: 978-1-6642-8432-6 (hc)
ISBN: 978-1-6642-8430-2 (e)

Library of Congress Control Number: 2022921623

Print information available on the last page.

WestBow Press rev. date: 12/20/2022

C O N T E N T S

ACKNOWLEDGEMENTS

First, I must thank God the Father, God the Son, and God the Holy Spirit for entrusting me with these insights. At YOUR Word, I submit this book to the public with the expectation of YOU fulfilling YOUR promise of lives changed, wisdom granted, and purpose realized and fulfilled for all who read it.

I am blessed with a wonderful, supportive family. To my parents, Jerrald and Christine Pierre: You have engrained within me and my siblings the importance of serving God and devoting our lives to HIS Work since childhood. Children cannot ask for a greater gift from their parents than this and we thank you so much for that. Thank you for the support, guidance, and love you have shown throughout our lives. We could not have accomplished what we have without your love and support. We were taught to let The Lord guide us and we pray that this is being carried out in our lives. Thank you for everything you have given. We are successful because of you. We love you!

To my amazingly sweet and equally silly siblings: Carmel Carter, Dr. Sharen Pierre-Waters, and Jerrald "Jay" Pierre, Jr. – Thank you all for taking this lifelong journey with me. I am blessed to have siblings who love and support one another throughout all of life's ups and downs and throughout the years that we have shared. It's been my honor and a privilege to call you my sisters and brother. Thanks for the fun times we continue to have whenever we are together. Gary, Joe, and Britney: I'm so glad that you were smart enough to marry into our family. Haha. You are my brothers and sister and I love you. Thank you. Thanks for being in our loving fam! To my wonderful nephews, nieces, and great-nephews, and great-nieces: Joey, Jefferey, Jeremy, Christyan, Gabe, Jasmine, Gideon, Cami, Zoey, Brooklyn, Jade, Ryan, Kailey Skye, & Chlobug – Tee-Tee loves you very much. It's been wonderful watching you all grow up and sprout kids and families of your own. Time passes quickly, doesn't it? Many of you are now in your 20s and 30s, yet I remember you all lying on my lap and ultimately ruining most of my clothes. I would not trade all of the memories and the time spent with you for anything in the world, although, it would be nice if you all stopped permanently "borrowing" my stuff! To my aunts, uncles, cousins, and our grandparents who are resting in The Lord: Thank you for the guidance, good times, and fun we have shared throughout the years. It was such an honor growing up with you as our guides and supporters. Without you all rearing us, we would not be where we are today. Thank you for embracing and uplifting us from childhood. Thank you for being a wonderful, supportive, crazy family. Thanks for all of the yummy food! Family, you have been my strongest supporters and my biggest inspiration. Thanks for a lifetime of love.

To my girls – Tonya, Wanda, Marcia, Ny'kiel, Monica, Whitney, Ms. Angel: Thank you for your love, prayers, support, and sisterhood throughout the years. God sends us friends who ultimately become family. That is my sentiments towards all of you! I love you all and I am grateful that God allowed you to be included in the story of my life. We've had lots of fun together, cried together, laughed together, and were outright crazy together. Thanks for all of it! I could not imagine life without you. You are a blessing to me. Much love to you, my sisters.

To my amazing colleagues and friends on the 5 Medicine PCU Nursing Team at Parkland Hospital in Dallas, Texas: You all continue to inspire me. I think of you daily and I pray that our relationship continues to grow as life moves forward. Thanks for being an awesome team! Thanks for the lives you touch and the people you serve. Their lives are better because of you. Keep leading and keep standing strong. Thank you for your service.

To my amazing WestBow Press team – Cameron Adamson, Angie Hibner, Joe Anderson, and the publishing and marketing team: Thanks for believing in me and being patient with me as I took this journey. Thank you for your guidance, your input, your advice, and your expertise. God bless you and I pray we are able to work together as a team for many more years.

To the readers of this book and all who I am blessed to know and love: Thank you for allowing me in your lives. I pray you are touched and blessed by this experience.

With Much Love & Adoration,
Trinette

P R O L O G U E

Reflect as You Progress

Who am I? How did I get here? How will I get to where I want to be? What do I need to do to change my present positioning to ensure future success? There are many questions that human beings ask regarding their life's journeys and the purposes they are intended to accomplish. While all questions may not be answered concurrently, asking and attempting to find answers to such questions shows a passion for more and the drive and initiative needed to move into a greater reality. This may be the case in personal, educational, spiritual, and professional avenues of life. This self-reflection process is one that some leaders use to better understand themselves in the pursuit of their goals and this process may lead to better self-awareness for those who are willing to take on the task.

Self-aware leaders often reflect on how their travels along life's journey carried them to present day positioning. Self-aware leaders understand that reflecting can be beneficial in understanding what made them who they are and how that understanding can benefit their future successes. Self-awareness is a key component of both business and personal relationships and may be integral to the successful navigation of life.

As we begin this learning process on leadership legacy, it is important to honestly and openly review the journey thus far. As we begin this "review of self" process, please ask yourself these questions:

- How did I get here?
- How has my past affected my present?
- How will my future be affected by my present?
- Where am I now versus where I aspire to be?
- How can I leverage my past and present beings to ensure I reach my goals in the future?

While you may not have answers to these questions at the beginning of chapter 1, the goal for this learning process is for you to uncover insights from your past and present that will assist you in being a more productive and successful leader. As you navigate through each section of this book, please keep these questions in the back of your mind. Write down your thoughts when you begin and record changes in your thought processes (if any) regarding your journey as you continue throughout this reflection and learning process. This is a learning, growth, and development initiative; therefore, please use this process to grow and strengthen your leadership prowess. I pray this book and this journey is a blessing that will positively affect your outcomes throughout the course of your life. Thank you for allowing me to travel this road of discovery with you.

PART I

Understanding Your Leadership Journey – How Did I Get Here?

"The past and the future are actually not so different. Every past event has a cause or causes that, as we look back and them, typically makes sense to us from our vantage point in the present. Likewise, each past event has implications and influences the events that follow it. It can be a very linear sequence that, again, make sense to us when we look back at them. To me, the future works in the exact same way. The difference, of course, is that we don't know what will happen in the future. Instead, we have a wide range of possible futures. But, just as with a singular event in the past, the events happening today, will shape the ultimate future." – Mike Ivicak, 2018.

As stated by Ian C. Woodward (2017), *"Leadership is a journey – not a destination."* This means we do not arrive at leadership and end our journeys. Leadership is continuous. Leadership is an ever-evolving, fluid, and continual learning process. Leaders do not reach a pinnacle and decide to settle in for the long haul. Leaders continue to move forward to build on what was accomplished in the past. This is because leaders know the importance of constant growth, continual development, and the incessant need to evolve in order to meet the ever-changing and dynamic needs of the world around us. This is evident in theories regarding leadership. Leadership theories and theoretical ideas of leadership have evolved, changed, and developed many times throughout the course of past decades. What the world once considered a style of great leadership is now seen as dictatorship. What we may have thought of as a type of "take charge and keep control" style of presenting is now considered micromanaging and authoritative mechanisms that turn followers against their intended leaders. Think back 5-10 years to the most popular leadership theory of that time. Many leadership theories have presented after that time and others will continue to bring knowledge and updated expertise to millions in the form of future leadership theories.

Just as leadership theories and the study of pertinent theorists continue to evolve and change over time, leaders themselves also evolve. Think about your leadership journey for a moment. When you began leading others, what was your approach? What was your mindset? If you had to choose a leadership style for your beginning days in leadership, what style would be chosen? What would others say about your early leadership moments? Thinking back on my own journey, I remember tasks I did, answers I gave, responses I uttered, and behaviors I portrayed that I would be embarrassed to admit to today. I remember thinking that I did not want to emulate those who were known as tyrants even though they were deemed "successful in business." Thankfully, I realized what needed to be changed and sought guidance on how to better my leadership prowess and presentation. I was blessed to encounter people along the way who were very transparent and open with me and those encounters helped steer me in the right direction as I continued along my career journey. Even as I reflect now, I chuckle at what we once thought was good leadership and how those tactics are now seen as negative in the workplace.

When we as leaders ponder where we are on life's journey, we must reflect on how we arrived at our current level of thinking, behaving, and developing. Such reflections can assist us with using lessons in our past to sculpt future successes. How did you arrive to this present moment in your leadership journey? What made you who you are? What actions or behaviors brought you from point A to subsequent points on your intended spectrum of leadership? How has what you believed at the beginning of life, throughout your collegiate journey, and during the previous years of your career evolved, changed, or shaped your current beliefs and practices? How has this affected where you hope to arrive next?

Knowing how the past affected us and what processes caused us to think and behave the way we do may be instrumental in helping us navigate how we will show up in the present and future. Let's take a moment to reflect on the journey of leadership throughout the continuum of life and career to get more insight into what made you unmistakably YOU. To begin this process, we must look into the past and reflect on where we started.

CHAPTER 1

Who I Was vs. Who I Am

"Life can only be understood backwards, but it must be lived forwards." - Søren Kierkegaard

The Formative Years – *"When I Grow Up..."*

Have you ever watched a group of children playing? Have you marveled at the boldness and reckless abandon that accompanies a child who is determined to do things that make adults cringe? As a child, you probably attempted to do a stunt that your parents or elder siblings deemed dangerous. While they cringed, you giggled with excitement. Without hesitation, you took the leap into areas where adults would not have imagined going because of the danger that seemed imminent. I shudder as I think of the days when I fearlessly did splits, flips, and my gymnastics dance routines on my make-shift balance beam (a.k.a., the top bar of my backyard swing set) as my mom urged me to "get down from there!" I was not afraid of what could happen. I fearlessly did back then what I would not attempt to do atop the bar of a swing set today.

Children are sometimes oblivious to danger. Many children seem to be absolutely fearless. Even if an unexpected tumble or fall results, it may take all of 2 seconds before a once crying or ailing child will be back at another attempt on conquering the dangerous stunts they set out to master. They are resilient. Children are determined to make their dreams a reality regardless of opposition or objection from others. If you have not experienced this level of determination, take a child to a store and try to remain sane as they repeatedly and incessantly state that their will to live solely hinges on you purchasing a candy bar or an action figure that they cannot live without (thanks to our retail marketers for strategically placing these temper tantrum-evoking items near checkouts where we are trying to quickly exit without our kids making a scene – tactical marketing at its best). You will witness that child-centric tenacity first hand on such a trip.

Have you experienced the beauty, determination, innocence, and simplicity in which children are surrounded when given the opportunity to express who they will be or where they expect they will end up as adults? Many of us know children who have fearlessly stated "I *will be* a superhero when I grow up," or "I *want to be* an astronaut when I grow up." Have you ever attempted to present "reality" to a child who is determined to be the next Spiderman, Black Panther, or Wonder Woman? If your experience was similar to mine, you were probably given multiple reasons as to why the goal of becoming the next superhero or superheroine was not an impossibility. You may have been given a plethora of reasons as to why becoming a superperson was the only suitable career path for your little loved one. You may have been one of the lucky ones who were given insight into the "coming soon upgrades" that the little prince or princess planned to implement to a popular superhero's superpowers that would work to better align with the current needs of society. For example, I've been told by a future superhero that kryptonite will not be a problem for the new breed of superheroes or superheroines because that little one has already (mentally) developed additional powers that would eliminate the negative effects of the substance on the bigger, better, and more improved superperson's powers. The science of it all…

While we may chuckle at the prospect of cartoon superheroes becoming a reality, the little ones stating these prospects are 100% sold into the idea. Strangely enough, many of us Have bought into the idea as well. This is evidenced by parents, aunts, uncles, grandparents, etc., hosting expensive superhero themed sleep overs and birthday parties. This becomes reality for the little ones when we buy capes, crowns, and costumes and ensure they stay in great wearing condition for the little superheroes, which may include us quickly and secretly replacing the costumes and extras when they show signs of wear and tear. I am certain that I am not alone in having the pleasure of sneaking the costumes off of a little one and washing them in the middle of the night as the superheroine slept. There is sometimes no other option that will keep us sane, right? Many of us have even called our little heroines by their assumed superheroine names to assist with bringing the superperson's dream to life. Although we know that the superheroine career path is not feasible or likely, for some reason, we are pulled into doing little things to uphold the belief; therefore, it becomes reality for the dreamer and questionable (at least on some level) for the adults witnessing the transformation. While I know that "Super Chlobug" or "Lightning Fast Ryan" will inevitably "save the day" in some business realms as adults, I realize that the cape and mask that they now wear will not be the daily business attire that is donned as they enter full-time occupations, yet I play along as expected. Do not judge me. I am sure there are capes or light sabers on display in your homes as well – and they may or may not belong to parents instead of the little ones. We are still allowed to pretend, are we not?

Watching a child dream of the future possibilities that may present in life is priceless. The little ones in our lives can invoke smiles, happy thoughts, and positivity as they relay with bubbling passion and unwavering belief the possibilities that they believe we cannot yet see. The conviction of little ones is palpable. It's also beautiful to witness for adults who may have lost that "I am fearless" mentality. I have looked on with awe as some of the little ones around me continued to relay the "yes, I can" determination that I remember touting many years ago.

For some adults, this child-like determination and conviction may still exist. Unfortunately for many, the childhood drive that boasts *"anything is possible if I imagine it"* does not continue throughout life's journey. For most of us, the childhood dreams and aspirations of being the greatest and best seemed to last only until our capes, princess gowns, and light sabers were passed to a younger sibling or donated to charity. Once these items were exchanged for "appropriate adult attire," we lost the passion that once led our dreams. Why is that?

Reflect back on your childhood years as you answer the following questions:

1. Who did you see as heroes or heroines when you were a child?
2. What did you want to be when you grew up?
3. Did you have a defining moment that caused you to believe that the dreams of your childhood years were incapable of becoming reality? If so, when was that moment and what caused the change in mindset?
4. In contrast, was there a defining moment that caused you to believe your dreams would be made reality as an adult? If so, when was that moment? What caused that determination to become your dominant mindset?

Leaders' Lesson

I would dare say all of us had dreams of following in the footsteps of someone we admired or doing something amazing when we were children. We have dreamt of leaving our mark on our world and positively influencing those around us. So, what changed? What caused those dreams to fall to the back of our psyches and dwindle away? What caused us to stifle our fearlessness and determination? Was it something that was said? Was it something that was experienced throughout our formative years that caused us to settle for less than we once believed was possible? What happened to turn our mantras from "I can do anything" to "I am forced to tolerate this job because I have bills?" When did settling for only what we are told we could achieve become mandatory? When did the wide-eyed belief that "anything is possible in my life" escape us? What happened to make us settle for "that's enough" instead of reaching goals no one else has reached?

While we may not be capable of becoming cartoon-based images of superheroes or superheroines, we are capable of making our childhood dream of being super a reality right where we are: In human form. We can use the dreams, determination, resiliency, vigor, and fearlessness that were apparent in our childhood years as a foundation on which we can build our future successes. What's stopping us?

For further thought:

1. How can we retain the characteristics and traits that made us resilient as children while we move throughout our careers?
2. How can we use what we were innately given and what we expressed as children to be more successful as adults and leaders?

Moving Into Adult Life – *"My Major Is…"*

"You have to know the past to understand the present." –
Carl Sagan

After navigating the world we knew as children, from toddlerhood to finishing senior high school, we gained insights into the world we were exposed to by parents, siblings, friends, and other loved ones. As we moved from the world of parents and family members guiding every step into the more independent practice of becoming adults and navigating college life, our views on who we are and what we believed may have also changed. What we considered becoming as children may have developed into another option as we entered young adulthood. For some, life's circumstances may have thwarted plans for us to attend college and we may have been forced to enter the workforce immediately after high school. Others may have planned to attain degrees after raising a family and settling into careers. Many of us had to take paths that we did not necessarily plan on taking. All of us have arrived where we are based on various situations, choices, and circumstances that we may not have been able to control.

For those who took the college route, think back to your aspirations of choosing a college or university. Reflect on how you felt as you took entrance exams and applied for the schools of your choice. Think back on what you wanted to be as you moved forward with choosing a major. Think about the first few months of college and how you felt when you realized that it may be tougher than you imagined. Did you experience periods of reality checks with regard to your chosen major and career choice? Did you experience periods of shock when you viewed your finances (or lack thereof)? What about your inventory of your dwindling food supply (e.g., your variety stash of Ramen Noodles)? How did you navigate meeting new people and attempting to acclimate to sharing your environment with strangers (e.g., your roommates)?

Think back to the realization and your feelings regarding other necessities of life previously provided for by parents or family members that were now your responsibility to manage. For some, these reflections may bring about happy feelings and chuckles as you remember that chicken-flavored Ramen Noodles rocked back then. For others, feelings of anxiety or trepidation may result as you think back on days when funds were low, stress was high, and anxiety was prevalent. Others may shake your heads as you think back on carefree times and how naivety made life appear sunny and light when compared to life as we now know it.

If we are honest, many of us can say that we did not expect the realities we were presented with during college life. For some, majors changed unexpectedly...multiple times. For others, our goals of becoming attorneys, educators, senators, business owners, healthcare providers, etc., became visible when we met phenomenal leaders in those fields. We wanted to emulate those individuals' careers and walk in the footsteps of those we deemed able to accomplish anything they set out to do. Regardless of what feelings result from your reflection on that time in your life, this was the period of time that ultimately influenced the path or direction in which you were headed.

Leaders' Lesson

Think on these questions as you reflect on the influences of your college/early adult years:

1. What was your intended career path prior to getting accepted into college or taking your first job?
2. What was your major on day 1 of college (if applicable)? Did it differ from the field of study you intended to pursue prior to acceptance into college?

3. How did your idea of what young adult life would be compare to what you experienced during that period of life?

4. Who were the key figures who framed your potential career or field of study? How did those influencers change your career outlook?

After reflecting on these questions, think about how your college or early adulthood years and lessons learned during that time can benefit you as a leader. The lessons learned during early adulthood can help us better understand the *"who am I"* and *"how did I get here"* that is integral to understanding where we are headed as leaders. Understanding where we came from, what shaped our beliefs and caused changes in our belief systems, and what preliminary actions we took to move us into the realm in which we currently find ourselves is key to understanding who we are and what made us.

CHAPTER 2

How Will My Present
Affect My Future?

"But just as with a singular event in the past, the events happening today will shape the ultimate future." – Mike Ivicak

Early and Mid-Career Navigation –
"This Isn't What I Intended!"

Disappointment Related to Degree Field vs Job

Working as a career coach is an area of particular interest to me. This is because I feel strongly that people need guidance throughout their careers, not only while in their high school or college years. For some reason, most professions do not offer this guidance outside of the mentor/mentee relationship that many are not privileged to attain. Although this is a venue where career choices can be discussed, this may not be the method of expert direction needed to gain insights into appropriate career choices, intended fields of study, and how to meet future goals of gaining access into certain career realms. The process of guiding individuals through disappointments in intended versus actual career paths is integral to successfully navigating that disappointment. For individuals seeking to make sense of their chosen path versus where they are currently positioned, career coaching and guidance is usually a great option.

One of the most common aspects of career coaching is done with early careerist candidates (those under the age of 40 or those with limited years' experience in their chosen career workforce). Many early careerists contact career coaches seeking advice and guidance on how to move forward with reaching their intended career goals out of frustration, usually after they realize that their careers are not going in the direction they planned. As was experienced by previous generations, many of these individuals graduate college and are not able to find work in the field of study in which they spent years learning vital material. Many complain that they spent four years or more working towards something that may never be reality. Early careerist clients make statements such as, "I have a degree in microbiology, but I am working as a receptionist at an IT company! Did I waste my time and money going to college?" Others quickly become disgruntled with their positioning within companies (e.g., working on the frontlines for multiple years when they planned to be in the Chiefs' Suite within 3 years post-degree attainment – true story). This lack of intended upward momentum becomes a harsh reality for many.

According to the University of Washington (2021), approximately 53% of college graduates are either unemployed or working in fields that do not require degrees. This means that more than ½ of recent college graduates are not able to find work in their fields of study. Around 26% of degree holders said they would change majors to pursue their passions if given the opportunity to repeat the college experience. Another 25% said they would change majors to better align their careers with better job opportunities (Hess, 2020). Is there any wonder as to why many early careerists ponder the effectiveness of their degrees or question if they chose the wrong field to enter? One thing is certain: Those who wonder if their career choice was a good one are not alone.

Take a moment to think back to your early and mid-careerist phases. There may be successes and perceived failures that you recant as you think on this time of your life. The successes may have been soon forgotten or may have propelled you to continue moving forward on the path you initially intended to travel. Those successes may have catapulted your career in the "right" direction or may have caused you to attain goals that you never dreamed imaginable. Think on those successes routinely and regularly and continue to build on that foundation of insights and wins gained to propel greater accomplishments and future achievements.

For those of us who have painstakingly navigated the early careerist phase of life, we may identify with some of the sentiments regarding early disappointments mentioned above. Many of us had high hopes for our careers and expected to quickly transcend the heights of those who came before us by making our marks on our professions within a short period of time. Others planned to retire from the "rat race" within the mid-careerist phase by saving money and ultimately starting our own businesses. Still others had dreams of running the reputable organizations we worked for within a *"maximum timeframe"* of 5-7 years after of graduating college. While our hopes and intentions were admirable, many of us found ourselves working in unintended positions, unfamiliar fields, and unwanted places for more years than we care to remember. For many, the hope of becoming an executive in an organization solely based on our drive, merit, degrees, and achievements may have been thwarted by a clique-based culture of "who you know; not what you know." Others of us had the unfortunate experience of being in the presence of those who voted or talked against us instead of supporting us simply because of what we looked like, how we identified, or what they perceived us to be based on what is visible on the outside. Others may have found out the hard way that some were intimidated by our drive, passion, strength, and expertise and at their envious hands we were held captive at levels we knew we surpassed and outgrew long ago. For a select few, the story is that we were able to work in fields that we intended and studied to master. Some very blessed individuals were given the opportunities earned and were able to quickly achieve the lofty goals set at the onset of their college careers. Regardless of the scenario with which we identify, we can use all of the past emotions, hopes, dreams, prospects, successes, and yes, even the disappointments, to keep propelling us forward.

Acclimating to the Real World – Working Through the Disappointment

> *"Once you embrace unpleasant news, not as negative but as evidence of a need for change, you aren't defeated by it. You're learning from it."* – Bill Gates

It seems easy to say, *"Let's use the pain to grow!"* That may be easy to do for a hard core personal trainer who seems to find joy in pushing clients beyond their limits to unending levels of pain, but for those of us who live in the real world where we are forced to remember the hurt and sometimes intentional negativity each time we walk into the workplace, it's not as easy to do. Many are constantly reminded of the stagnation that resulted when we encounter those who may have purposefully placed our careers in a state of frozen animation while we were forced to watch those around us with less experience, less education, less accolades, and less effectiveness being promoted without merit. If we are honest, we know of someone who has been placed in positions that they did not earn. We all know those who have been set up to succeed and those who were given opportunities they had not earned simply because of who they knew. Being able to say that you are that person takes even more honesty and self-reflection.

One wise phrase that has been reiterated throughout the ages and will continue to be true until the end of Earth's history is *"life is not fair."* Those of us who have navigated this life for decades may now add to that phrase *"…and people will not always treat you fairly, remember what you did for them, or praise your hard work and dedication."* Let's look at how this truth has presented throughout history.

If we recall the Biblical account of the 10 lepers who Jesus healed on a road to Jerusalem (Luke 17:11-19), we can see these statements come to life. Although these 10 lepers were shunned by society and seen as sinful, evil, and thus deserving of their debilitating and shameful diseases, Jesus took time to speak to and ultimately heal those who were banished to live outside of city limits because they were "unclean." After being approached by the lepers, Jesus gave instruction for them to go into the city and show themselves to the priests (this was a Jewish custom that ensured the processes of verification of healing and the performing of purification rites to take place after one was made "clean"). Out of the 10 lepers who were healed on their way to show themselves to the Jewish priests, only one individual returned to thank Jesus for the miracle He performed. Jesus asked, *"Didn't I heal ten men? Where are the other nine?"* (Luke 17:17 NLT). This was a good question…and a great learning moment for all humanity.

Another Biblical account may mirror the experiences of those who have faced disappointments by the hand of others and through little to no fault of their own. The story of Joseph in Genesis (chapters 37-50) shows us that those we thought loved and supported us may sometimes fail us and even sell us out. Joseph's God-gifted talents were envied, downplayed, and used against him. His brothers plotted to kill him, but God had other plans. Joseph was ultimately sold into slavery by his brothers (those who he worked alongside and with whom he lived in close communion) and he was taken to a foreign land where he never planned to end up (an alternate road than the road he planned to travel). Joseph had purpose and was blessed in all he did. Even as a slave in Egypt, he ran Potiphar's (a high ranking official with close proximity to the Pharaoh of the land) house and was honored above his master's other servants and workers. Joseph was given high position only to have his honor and position taken away at the hand of someone who could not force him to do wrong. Joseph was falsely accused of disrespecting and inappropriately interacting with Potiphar's wife when he continued to spawn her inappropriate advances. Joseph was thrown into a damp, wet pit with other prisoners and was forgotten by those he helped be successful during his time serving in Potiphar's court.

You may think, "Well, that is a horrible story and it does not give much hope to those who are stuck in a rut and forced to settle for less than they have earned. Who wants to be thrown off course for many years before being given a shot?" At first glance, this is a valid question, but there is more to the story of Joseph's life….just as there is more to our stories. Here's what happened next: While in the dungeon (or at the place where others may have thought Joseph was at his lowest), Joseph began gaining insights into his life by leaning on God for guidance, wisdom, and knowledge. While he was in a place that was dark, cold, and reeked of putrid smells, he decided to allow himself to be used to serve others. God was able to hone and perfect Joseph's abilities, his skills, and his insights to prepare him for his next opportunity and his intended purpose.

While in the dungeon prison, Joseph met two individuals who needed his talents to understand where they were in life. Joseph was gifted with a special inclination to interpret dreams. Joseph interpreted troubling dreams for the two prisoners who needed insight into their futures. Joseph took time to reach others while in his lowest place and he helped others even when he did not see a return on his investment. Even when he was at his lowest, Joseph still worked in purpose. He helped those who found themselves needing guidance while he was in his lowly place. Joseph continued to do what he knew was right and just, even though many around him mistreated and abused him. He had the opportunity to give into the temptation to do wrong when few were watching, but he continued to do what was right. He continued to help others. Joseph could have wallowed in self-pity and complained about his circumstance to whoever would listen. He could have refused to help others and focus on his misery. Joseph decided to be positive even in a very undeserving situation. That determination to do right even when things looked grim gave Joseph favor with the prison guard and all of the prisoners he encountered. His positive outlook set him up for greatness. Unfortunately, for all of his good work, support, and dedication to those he encountered while in the dungeon, Joseph was forgotten once those he helped was allowed to return to Pharaoh's service. This lapse in memory by those Joseph had blessed in the dungeon where he was held prisoner spanned the course of two long years. Now, if I were Joseph, I may have decided to hold back my gifts and decide to let those needing help find another source of guidance, but that was not Joseph's outlook. Joseph decided to continue to work in purpose and give to others. Even when it seems he was forgotten and neglected by humans who could control his path, he continued to serve. God never forgot about Joseph because Joseph remained true to who he was and faithful to The Lord.

The end of the story: Joseph's interpretations of the dreams of others became reality and this set him up for success. For two years, Joseph remained in the dark, damp, hopeless place (this is a metaphor for some of our current situations), but his influence and helpfulness was remembered at the right moment. One of the men Joseph helped through his gift of dream interpretation was the cup bearer for Pharaoh. Pharaoh was haunted by horrible dreams for multiple nights. No one in his court could interpret the dream.

This was a typical set up for a God who has a plan for us that far exceeds human negativity and mortal control. It was then that the cup bearer remembered Joseph's gift and told Pharaoh about Joseph. The result: Joseph was summoned by Pharaoh, the king of Egypt, to assist with a problem that no one else could solve. Through God's guidance, Joseph was able to use his skills and his abilities to meet Pharaoh's need, which ultimately led to him being placed in a high-raking position. The same talents or gifts that others ridiculed and belittled throughout the earlier years of Joseph's life became the driving force that allowed him to work in Pharaoh's court as the Second-In-Command in Egypt. The place of his captivity ultimately became the place of his greatest triumph and spearheaded his orchestration of sustaining many nations during a time of predicted famine and widespread loss. This included sustaining and protecting those who abused, ridiculed, and sold him out.

How can these stories be applied to our lives? How can we relate to these instances and glean leaders' lessons from them? We can prepare ourselves for better days even when the outlook is dim. When we feel that we are being held back or held down at the hands of others who mean us harm, these are times when we should hone our skills, continue to live and work in our intended purpose, and serve others while we wait for the door to our next blessing to be opened.

For those of us who may have had our hopes and dreams thwarted by the malicious intent of others or if we did not receive the praise, recognition, and thanks we earned, the lesson is apparent: Work hard at continuing to build your dreams even when others attempt to downplay or curb your abilities. As many of us may have realized by now, some of our peers, managers, and executives may not openly appreciate or acknowledge who we are and what we are capable of achieving. They may not return to us to say "great job" after we have presented solutions that saved the company from losing clients. Others may intentionally rebut every idea, suggestion, or insight that we offer. Others may maliciously use our ideas and expertise to gain unearned praise from those they are attempting to impress. The story of Joseph gives insight into what many of us have learned throughout years past: We may not be praised for all of our successes. We may not be shown support by those intended to uphold and uplift us. We may not be remembered or thanked by all we have helped to gain insights, by those we assisted in finding their way in our organizations, or for times when we lent a hand to help others become successful. We may not have those who are intimidated by our accomplishments and achievements award us with higher positions, more appropriate salaries, or better opportunities for success. Unfortunately, this disappointment is a part of our human experience. It is not always earned, but often gifted without remorse from those may not mean us well. This lesson is hard learned during the early careerist phase and reiterated for some throughout the entirety of the career journey. Please know that this is not the end of the story...unless we succumb to it. Will it hurt? Yes. Will it be tough? Yes. Is it doable? Absolutely, it is. We can learn from these negative experiences and resolve to continue to live in purpose and do what we know we have been designed to do.

Leaders' Lesson: Setting Up for My Next Move

The question becomes "How do we use the difficult lessons learned during early and mid-careerist phases of our careers to help us grow and develop?" Others may attempt to give insight into your story and may attempt to dictate how it should read, but only you hold the pen. No one can write your story unless you give up the power to do so. As I often tell my student, mentees, and those who I am blessed to encounter throughout my life's journey, *"We sometimes give too much power to others who are outside of our lives looking in. You are the only person who can dictate where the punctuation of your life's story will be placed. You decide if disappointments are ended with commas or periods. Will you allow discouragement, unfair treatment, and disappoint to derail your path or will you push forward? No one has the power to write your story…unless you grant it to them. Others are players in the game of your life, but you hold the controller that dictates your life's moves."* While these words are often shared with those I encounter in a personal and professional setting, these words also force me to remember the same. Please share them with those you love and repeat them to yourselves often.

You must decide whether you will settle into others' beliefs regarding who you are and what you are worth or if you will fight with all of your might to reach your goals regardless of opposition from others. Will you remain in purpose or allow the mumblings of others to hold you back? Please meditate on the quote below as you reflect on disappointments or discouraging moments you may have faced during your career.

> **"Career shocks are events that set a process in motion. They offer an opportunity for both personal and [professional] development. This is not to deny the fact that they are painful and can be, for a certain period of time, disorienting. The important point is this: you are at the beginning of a process that can be an opportunity for new perspective"** (Butler, 2017).

Again, this quote is easier read than stomached, especially for those of us who have stayed awake at night wondering if we would ever rise from the ashes that others piled on top of us. Although painful to admit, the words in the quote above are true. People who are comfortable or content where they are will rarely make changes that will cause a drastic change in their environment or situation. There must be a catalyst or push given to invoke actions that lead to the will to change course.

One thing that we learned during the COVID pandemic is that necessity truly is the mother of invention. During the pandemic, there were many who lost their jobs as a result of decreased demand for human labor. Many industries halted or significantly decreased their services, which resulted in massive layoffs and skyrocketing unemployment rates. Because of that loss, some of the affected individuals began seeking alternatives to working for others. Some opened their own start-up businesses and were able to employ those seeking work. Others found that their hobbies or hidden talents could be showcased on social media sites resulting in income opportunities.

According to the Census Bureau (2021), in July 2020, the number of applications for new business startups reached an all-time high of 4.4 million in the United States, which accounted for a 95% increase from data pulled at the same time in 2019. Japan registered 84,000 new businesses from the start of the pandemic through October 2020. The United Kingdom reported a 30% increase in registered companies by November 2020. We must wonder if any of these statistics would be fact if there was not a prevalent need to seek out other means of monetary gain. The drive needed to propel these entrepreneurs forward was the negative outcome of becoming unemployed or the reality that there were alternatives for working for others in a 9-5-scheduled job role. With many dealing with changing home responsibilities, children being home schooled, and decreasing income for some households, alternatives were sought by some. These individuals used the negatives set in their paths to make positive moves in their careers. While all businesses that began in 2020 may not have been successful, the steps were taken to start businesses because of the drive to survive dire circumstances.

Think back to how you felt after experiencing a career disappointment or after being unable to find a position in your intended career path. Did those feelings cause you to surrender to the details of the moment or did you become so uncomfortable with where you were that you began revising your 5-year plan to align with better outcomes? Were you determined to use the negative behaviors of others, the lack of appreciation within your organization, or the lack of opportunity to grow your career to fuel better outcomes for your future? Did you buy into what others thought of your capabilities or did you resolve to press forward with greatness in mind regardless of the negativity of others?

Years ago, one of my colleagues was given unsolicited feedback from his direct manager. After giving a presentation regarding a new initiative that went against a previously instituted process, his manager informed him that he shuffled while he presented, he used the sound, "umm…" too frequently, and his use of humor during what should have been a serious presentation was "off-putting for *all* who attended." A short time after the meeting, this colleague was contacted by some of the organization's executives who attended the meeting. He was openly praised for his contribution to the strategic goals of the organization. The executives were so impressed with his presentation that he now sits at the same conference room table and at the same job level with the person who attempted to give "constructive criticism" after his presentation. Strangely enough, what my colleague presented went against the recommendation that his former manager submitted to the executives, which may have prompted the list of negatives presented by that manager on his behalf. While one criticized with mal-intent, others elevated his efforts and ultimately his position.

While each story may not end this way, we can learn a lesson from this situation. Even when your ideas are not popular or your methods of presenting do not align with the approval of some who believe in "the way I do it is law," keep pushing forward. Keep showing up and keep fighting for what you want. Use the negatives in your career as a learning process. See the difficulties and failed attempts as instances that promote growth and invoke changes that will result in better outcomes.

The determination to push forward in the midst of turmoil has led many leaders to greatness. The hunger and passion for reaching goals, even when others deem us failures or unworthy, has been the fuel many needed to push toward success. Take for example some of those who have forever changed our world because of their drive and determination and their incessant refusal to accept "no" as the final answer. Many of those individuals were rejected or labeled as failures prior to entering their success. Here are a few examples of "no" turning into greatness:

> *Jesus Christ* – Jesus is the ultimate example of someone who was ridiculed, rejected, underappreciated, and undermined by those who were busy being jealous of Him instead of embracing Him for Who He was while on Earth. While some drew close to Him, others spent their time attempting to belittle and berate Him. In the end, Jesus performed the miracle of miracles in the form of saving the world through His unselfish Gift – His Life. With or without the backing of those who felt they were the authority of His time, Jesus achieved greatness on a level the world has never seen since and will never experience again from those walking this Earth.

> *King David (Ancient King of Israel)* – Before his rise to fame, young David was rejected and ridiculed by family, monarchs, and those who should have supported him. David was told by King Saul that he was "JUST" a boy and he could not win the battle over seemingly larger than life giant who had trained for combat since he was old enough to walk. To add insult to injury, David's eldest brother (who was receiving help from David at the time – a very interesting insight) belittled David's contribution to

his family by asking about the "few sheep" that David was responsible for shepherding. Even though David's contribution as a shepherd was integral to his family's livelihood, his brother attempted to downplay David's role. *Key point: Be careful of those who try to belittle your talents and contributions. This is envy and intimidation at its best.* Regardless of the negativity of the king and his family, David was determined to follow what God told him – not what human beings who were not self-aware and were jealous of him relayed. David pushed forward and did something that no one else (including an entire Israelite army that was trained to engage in combat) could do. He used what he trained to do in a time when no one was watching him to ultimately change the course of history for his nation. *Bonus point: Eventually, the same king who belittled his abilities became the man David would replace on the throne (1 Samuel 17:1-54).*

Albert Einstein – The man most noted as "intelligent" did not have a fast start in life. Mr. Einstein would go on to stun the world with his equations and research that pioneered physics as we know it, but he was initially deemed "mentally deficient" at a young age. As a child, he did not speak until the age of 4, did not read until the age of 7, which was far behind those in his developmental group. Mr. Einstein did not let others labeling him as "mentally challenged" keep him from greatness. The world benefitted as a result of his tenacity and his ability to ignore what was said about him by those he encountered.

Sir James Dyson – Dyson attempted and failed to invent over 5,100 prototypes of the Dyson Vacuum before building the prototype that would generate over $4.5 billion.

J. K. Rowling – The author of the widely-known *Harry Potter* series was a divorced, depressed, single mother on welfare prior to writing novels that made her one of the richest women in the world. When asked about her early days prior to reaching success, Rowling stated, *"It is impossible to live without failing at something, unless you live so cautiously that you might as well not have lived at all – in which case, you fail by default."* This is a very valid insight.

Jerry Seinfeld – After being heckled and booed off stage by an audience as he froze in terror in front of in a comedy club, Mr. Seinfeld decided to either try again or return home and take a job in a field he did not like. He decided to try again the next night at the same comedy club. He gave an all-star performance on that stage...and the rest is history. Where would we be without *"The show about nothing?"*

Oprah Winfrey – As beloved as Ms. Winfrey now is, she was once fired from a television station where she held a job as an anchor. When reflecting on that seemingly failed attempt at becoming a household name, Ms. Winfrey stated, *"There is no such thing as failure. Failure is just life trying to move us in another direction."* Those words yield great insight for those who are faced with disappointment. Needless to say, Ms. Winfrey's $3 billion+ empire is a stark example of the drive to success in the face of rejection yielding amazing results.

Walt Disney – After being told by his former editor that his characters "lacked vision and imagination," Walt Disney went on to begin an empire that long outlived the man himself. Imagine life without Disney World, Mickey Mouse, Disney+, etc. Many parents owe their sanity to the work of this visionary legend. Regarding failure, Mr. Disney stated, *"I think it's important to have a good hard failure when you're young... because it makes you kind of aware of what can happen to you. Because of it I've never had any fear in my whole life when we've been near collapse and all of that. I've never been afraid."*

Elvis Presley – The night he performed the first time on the Grand Ole Opry stage (after which he was promptly fired), Elvis was told, *"You ain't goin' nowhere, son. You ought to go back to drivin' a truck."* Elvis decided to throw away the keys to the truck and try again. Elvis became famous throughout the world for doing the very thing he was told he would never be successful at doing. Can you imagine life without some of his iconic hits? Thankfully, he did not allow naysayers to derail his quest for success.

Michael Jordan – After being cut from his high school basketball team, Michael Jordan continued to practice and hone his skill. After winning numerous championships and a plethora of MVP titles, he is now arguably one of the greatest players (if not the greatest) to ever touch a basketball. Mr. Jordan said, *"I have missed more than 9,000 shots in my career. I have lost almost 300 games. On 26 occasions I have been entrusted to take the game winning shot, and I missed. I have failed over and over and over again in my life. And that is why I succeed."* Notice that Mr. Jordan took note of his past failures and used those to propel him to his current status.

Stephen King – Remember the movie *"Carrie"* and how we shrunk down in our seats as we watched that crazed prom queen terrorize high school students during that horror film? If it was not for the determination, drive, and persistence of Stephen King, we would not have experienced that movie or countless others that have been sold out to audiences around the world. Strangely enough, Mr. King's book, *"Carrie"* was rejected by 30 publishing companies before he (at the insistence of his wife) revamped the book. As a result, the book was accepted for publishing and movie rites were also brought to the bargaining table. Mr. King also has a book entitled *"On Writing"* which was fueled by his experience and lessons learned during his career that is currently considered the gold standard for aspiring writers.

There are many more stories of individuals who did not let initial failure or rejection stop them from reaching their goals. While all stories may not end in billion dollar empires, some may. Who knows what outcomes those who press forward will see? Either we can succumb to the rejection brought forth by others and decide to sit in despair or we can take those same failures, mold them into lessons, and use them to make us stronger and more determined to succeed. We have the power write our stories – not those who reject us; not our failures; not our disappointments. While these negative experiences affect our stories, they do not dictate our outcomes. We do. How will your story read?

CHAPTER 3

How do I Embrace Who I Am by Leverage ME into My Future Successes

"Transformation is a process, and as life happens there are tons of ups and downs. It's a journey of discovery." – Rick Warren

To be successful in life, we must take the good and the bad and use each to grow. How can we use the lessons from the past and what we are currently doing to ensure great outcomes in the future? How can we use our foundational beliefs, norms, and experiences to grow and transform ourselves into leaders that others will emulate and talk about for years to come? We must leverage what we know about ourselves to build our future success. In the previous chapter, we discussed how to use failures, disappointments, and hurt to our advantage. We can use these situations to motivate us to do better. While often difficult to do, reviewing and embracing your past failures can be both cathartic and revolutionary. This process is often used by those who are deemed successful because it keeps them grounded and motivated to continue to succeed. This same practice is needed if we are to fully understand who we are and where we are going. Let's take a deeper look at how we can discover ourselves, learn about ourselves, and use what we discovered as a foundation for future success.

Leveraging ME into Success: How to Get From Here to There

> *"We have two options in life - Change or settle. If you don't like where you are, change your location. If you don't like who you are, become someone you will adore. Don't settle for less than what you know you can accomplish. If you decide to settle, don't complain about the outcome - embrace it."* – Dr. Trinette Pierre

The theme thus far has centered on the need to understand and embrace who we are if we want to know where we are headed. Without this insight and knowledge, we are not viewing ourselves in the truest form of who we are and thus we cannot fathom who we are meant to become. Once we understand what made us who we are, we can build on that foundation.

How do we get from where we are to where we want to be? Reflect...then take action to make it happen. Reflecting without action is fruitless; therefore, action must follow the reflection if we wish for success to be our destination. What would happen if a football team reviewed the highlights from a Sunday night game that they lost, yet did not revise their game plan or practice perfecting the areas where mistakes were noticeably made? Nothing would happen! The outcome would be the same. Failure would continue to result. Individuals, teams, or companies who continue to perform the same actions in the same manner while expecting different outcomes are displaying insanity. We must take different action to change outcomes. All input is not bad input that is intended to derail us. We must consider the source of the input, the relationship with those giving that input, and the intent of the relaying party before making a decision on how to proceed. These are critical points to consider prior to deciding on the next move. Some input is well-intentioned advice that may be used to propel us forward. Other input may be intended to belittle, berate, or stifle us. Each individual must carefully examine the source of the messages being relayed and plan accordingly.

Revisit some of the questions we pondered in the previous chapters and think on the insights that you uncovered regarding your past. The next step is moving forward with either continuing to grow on what has made you successful or revising your plan to ensure better outcomes in the future. Write down the key insights you gained from the previous chapters. Think on the failures or successes you identified. For each failure either: a) Decide to keep moving forward by focusing on how to revive or revise that project, idea, invention, etc. or b) Table those ideas and move in a direction that is more suitable for goal attainment.

Option A: Revive or Revise – Failure does not necessarily mean the idea or innovation was not a good prospect. There may be some steps that you need to take to make the idea, invention, or proposal more viable and worthy of review for your intended audience. Again, examine the source and the intent of the person giving feedback before considering the next step. Let's again consider the book *"Carrie"* by Stephen King. Although the book obviously had great bones or a great foundation, there were changes that needed to be made for it to reach its full potential and become a successful endeavor for the publishing companies Mr. King approached with his idea. We may not need to scrap all ideas and processes simply because the intended audience did not accept or cosign the idea the first time it was presented. We may need to revise or revive what was offered and realign our product with the need of the industry or intended audience. There are various steps that can be taken to conduct this process, the easiest is a Biblical principle that applies to life as well as business: *Ask – Seek – Knock*

(Matthew 7). At each step of this process, we have the option of staying to fight for the successes we know we will achieve or fleeing to move on in another direction.

Ask - You Will Never Know if You Never Ask!

One simple way of knowing why others were not receptive to our ideas is to ask for feedback and constructive criticism from the intended audience and key stakeholders we wish to target. We have the options of either asking for insight to assist us with reaching better outcomes or taking the failure at face value and going in another direction. Asking for a quick conversation regarding what could be done to better align with the individual's, group's, or organization's strategic plan, goals, outcomes, etc. may assist us in revising and realigning our processes, product, and ideas. While some key stakeholders may not be willing to take the time to participate in this process, this will not be the case in all instances. Many leaders will give the feedback needed to produce better outcomes if we engage them. Unfortunately, this process may require some inward changes and a bit of comfort in approaching others to discuss something that we may have taken as a slight or negative input, but this process may be integral to our successes. We will have to put aside the hurt and shame that accompany disappointments or untoward feedback to accomplish this task. Going to those we feel have intentionally or unintentionally hurt or harmed us is not easy. We have to resolve to swallow our pride, put aside the defensive nature that we as human beings use to protect ourselves in such situations, resist the urge to fight back or rebut everything that is stated, and move forward with the *"what can happen if I do this…"* in mind.

Think about the potential for success that may present if you ask those intended to accept your product to give insight into what you should do to better align with their needs or the needs of their customers. Think about the success that could follow if you could put aside the harsh exterior that follows disappointment and reflect on the information gained from the "ask" interaction. The "ask" may be the key to opening that door to success that you thought was forever closed to you. Also, taking this initiative may prompt those stakeholders you wish to capture to be more receptive to your idea after changes have been made as suggested. Your tenacity and willingness to grow from the interaction may work in your favor. While this takes some swallowing of pride to accomplish, the results may be worth the effort.

Seek – Keep Searching for What You Want!

After obtaining information from those who are willing to give insight into what should be revised or changed in order for you to reach success, seek out ways to achieve the presented insights. While some of the insights given may be simple tweaks that require very little effort, other insights may require more work on the part of the receiver. For example, if you are told that you did not get a promotion because of the lack of certifications, lack of expertise, need for increased exposure or knowledge, etc., contemplating ways to grow in these areas may be the answer. For some, this may be the place where you decide to go in an alternate direction. For example, someone who has attained numerous degrees, certifications, etc., may not be open to hearing he needs an additional 4-year degree to earn entrance into a particular sector of business. For some, seeking an additional opinion may be the next move. Others may wish to table the idea and seek another course of action. Those individuals may resolve to accept the failure and take another route to reaching success. Everyone's opinion of what should occur after receiving such input from the intended audience is individually focused. The next move would have to be decided on a personal level.

For others, you may be so dedicated to reaching the goal you have set for yourself and your career that you decide to take the advice and move forward with seeking out ways to incorporate that advice into your practice. This may require revising the "5-year plan," moving to another company, changing occupations, earning additional degrees, etc. Those who wish to stay and fight are more inclined to believe in their ideas, innovations, and proposals and will keep pushing forward no matter what obstacles present. Those are the individuals who will do whatever is needed to make their dreams a reality. They will not accept "no" as the final answer. These individuals are not willing to accept anything less than success for their plan or idea.

The choices are to seek out what is needed to promote future success or retreat and eliminate the initial idea, innovation, or plan. The key is deciding which path is meant for you to take. Not everyone is willing to take or meant to take the steps required to revise or revive previous ideas or plans that did not produce expected outcomes. The choice is very individualized and personal. Only you can decide which route is best for you and your plan to attain your set goals.

Knock – Keep Fighting for What You Want!

One of the themes of leadership is to keep pushing forward. Leaders know that success may not come to all on the first attempt, but with determination, will, skill, drive, faith, and passion, *it will happen*. Those who are determined to reach success do not succumb to failure the first time…or second…or third time failure rears its ugly head (e.g., Sir Dyson is a great example of this). Those who are determined to succeed continue to make calls, send emails, show up at events, and look for opportunities to knock down the barriers that stand between them and success. For many, the need to continue the fight, continue knocking, and continue revamping and revising causes disdain and discontentment. This ultimately leads to some deciding to surrender their potential for success to those who deem them unworthy of the opportunity.

Unfortunately, these individuals resolve to abandon their hopes and dreams to buy into the notion that others dictate and control their futures. For those who feel this is not the route they wish to travel, they knock. They continue to knock until someone opens the door. Being told that they are not visionaries or that they lack imagination (e.g., Walt Disney) does not compute to this group of people. Standing in a conference room where they are met with unfriendly stares, critical jeers, and even laughs at them (not with them) will not deter this group (e.g., Jerry Seinfeld). Being told they do not fit "the look" of leaders does not phase this group of people (e.g., Oprah Winfrey). Losing a job and being told they do not qualify for other positions within the company does not mean their careers should end. This group of knockers and fighters take the feedback as building blocks that will eventually lift them up to their Divinely-ordained level of success.

If one person says "no," keep knocking on doors. If your current boss does not believe in you, keep fighting for other opportunities. If you hear, "that won't work for us," keep looking for a different way to make it happen. "...and to everyone who knocks, the door *will* be opened" (Matthew 7:8, NLT). Please note: These words by Jesus do not reflect, "if you knock once, the door shall be opened." Although once may be enough to get doors open in some instances, there may be times that you must continue to press for the desired outcomes to become reality. This is where faith and diligence come into play. You may have to work for what you want and continue trusting even when things seem unlikely to result the way you wish, but with perseverance and vigilance, the knock will get answered.

Case in point: How many times do sales representatives knock on your front door before retreating? If you are like me, you have listened to the door bell ringing for more than 5 minutes at a time on consecutive days (usually during dinner time) before the agent attempting to sell pest control services is allowed to give the face-to-face pitch that you have heard many times before. You can state that you already have great service and are in the middle of family dinner, but is that enough to make the representative decide to leave your front porch? That's probably not the case. If it is, that person is probably not the best salesperson. The usual reply is, *"I'm not going to take up much of your time because I know you are having dinner, but how much is the current service charging you? I actually signed up some of your neighbors who were not satisfied with their current service. I am sure we can beat your current company's prices and give more comprehensive service for the spiders, mice, and mosquitos that we know are highly active in your area. As I walked up to your door, I noticed there are spider webs and other concerning nests surrounding your home's easements. That's something we can take care of quickly and efficiently for you and I can start the work today so we can get it under control quickly before the summer's peak in bug activity. What we offer is…"* The *"no, thank you"* responses that we give out repeatedly to ensure we can quickly return to our dinner that is getting colder by the second are usually met with fast-turnaround rebuttals and more tenacity. After being worn down enough to listen or in an attempt to simply end the conversation that has worked to cross our eyes in despair, we ask if we can get a pamphlet, business card, or a web address we can visit to gather more details. If the representative is really ambitious (as my sales visitors usually are), they'll say something like, *"actually I don't have a business card, but I can walk the property with you now and we can look at potential costs of XYZ services that I see you need."* If that does not work, the next move is usually, *"I can email you some information or call you with more details. What is the best number or email address that I can use to contact you?"* The reps can be relentless in their pursuits. Their objective is to keep pushing even if opposition presents.

Another scenario: Say you did not answer the door after the incessant knocking event. Even if the representative does retreat because no one knocked, home owners will always know they were there on porches. The sales people leave their business cards, pamphlets outlining services they offer, or a simple sticky note with their contact information including the promise of "I'll be servicing homes in your neighborhood again tomorrow and will stop by around 6pm." Tenacious! They refuse to let one unopened door stop them from attempting to be successful. There is a level of respect for their tenacity that must be granted, even if the outcome is the listener must endure ongoing sales pitches.

Why do we not follow this example of vigilance and diligence that sales representatives exhibit? Although some may cringe when encountering sales representatives, we can learn a lot from these individuals' drive for success. All of us should emulate the tenacity of the pest control salespeople of the world: Keep pushing forward to ensure you do not remain stagnant or dwell in the place of defeat. Keep revising, keep revisiting, keep insisting, and keep knocking. Do not let the first *"no, thank you"* be the determining factor of your success. Most of all, keep believing in yourself. Trust in what you know you can do regardless of naysayers or those who may knock you down in the pursuit of your purpose. Keep getting back up...and keep knocking on doors. Your success is only as prevalent as your drive...and your knock.

Option B: Scrap, Retreat, and Surrender

The fight does not appeal to everyone. There are many who are not equipped to fight for success. There are others who are not destined to be leaders. There are defining moments that work to identify those who are designed for the fight and those who are not cut out for the pain and hurt that accompanies the struggle that is sometimes required to reach lofty goals. The fight is not for everyone. The path may not be easy. The road to your idea of success may be riddled with potholes, snakes, bandits, and inclement weather. Each individual has to decide if the prize is worth the tumultuous journey.

Going back to my career coaching engagements, there are times when a client feels retreat is the best option. I have witnessed many clients who attempted to move into higher positions quickly give up after being told they would *"never* be management-level material" by someone who was supposed to be a "leader." When I asked what these clients would do to better prepare for their next promotion (this question was presented in an attempt to keep the clients positive and deflect the negative comments sent their way), some clients repeated what they were told by those causing the quick surrender. When those clients were asked, "what steps do you have in place to reach your goals," the prospect of revising or revisiting the plan and pushing forward was not remotely on the list. The defeatist attitude presented instead. Some of the responses from clients included, *"well, I don't have any other ideas," "that manager holds my career in her hands,"* and *"I don't care. I am done. I'll just keep working where I am."* Unfortunately, the beliefs and negativity of others seem to outweigh the passion and drive some of the clients had prior to the untoward and discouraging encounters. These clients allowed others to reroute their dreams and aspirations, which ultimately gave the naysayers the power to write someone else's story.

We know that the will to fight is not as strong in some as it is in others. This is alright. If our ultimate position is one of staying where we are, settling in, hunkering down, and weathering the storm without attempting to get to higher ground or a safer shelter, we must embrace that place and use it to our advantage. Many will never reach their potential, see their dreams become reality, or embrace all that they are created and purposed for simply because of negativity that prompts them to settle. Others will muster the will and determination to do whatever is necessary to fulfill their dreams, reach their goals, and live in their designed purpose. The fight is not for everyone and the scars may not be either. For those who are not designed to fight, embracing the place of resolve and contentment to ensure survival becomes their goal. Again, this is not necessarily a bad outcome. This may be their intended path that will lead them to their intended purpose. This may be where they feel more comfortable and they may excel in that place. The choice is very individual and very personal. Each of us must decide which path to take.

Leaders' Lesson: Fight or Flight?

Every person we encounter will not be designed, created, or destined to lead. Some are great at following and supporting leaders and this is their intended purpose. If everyone took the lead in a group, this could cause major issues. If churches has 300 pastors and no congregation to carry out the other duties of the ministry, how efficient and effective would those institutions be? If hospitals consisted of 200 chief officers yet no providers, nurses, engineers, environmental services workers, etc., the hospital would not be serving its intended purpose. Simply put, some are designed to lead others. Some are designed to follow and support others.

Some are not programmed to navigate the battles, the tears, the heartache, the complaints, the naysayers, and the disappointments that present before many of us reach our full potential and ultimately reach our goals. Failures work to identify what category to which we belong by showing how we react when we encounter setbacks, hurts, and disappointments. Some decide to take the early negatives as a depiction of the long-term forecast of their lives while others decide to use their negatives to grow and develop. While some cannot see beyond the temporary bruises to see what will come next, others focus on the thicker skin that will develop after the hurt heals. The key is finding out what category we belong to and, once this reality is identified, embracing it.

1. What obstacles or setbacks have influenced your present and future?
2. Have you experienced criticism (constructive or otherwise) feedback that caused you to question your path? What was the outcome?

3. How can you leverage the negatives and positives you have encountered and use those events to build a platform of future successes?

4. What can you begin doing today to help strengthen your positioning and success in the future?

Latent Careerist: Reflecting on ME

For those who are blessed to have reached the point where retirement and freedom from alarm clocks, monthly meetings, and traffic is near, congratulations. You have worked many years to get to this point and have navigated the ins and outs, ups and downs, and certainty and uncertainty of the business world. At this point in your career, you are looking towards getting your business house in order in preparation for your joyous and smile-ridden exit from the workplace. During your final weeks to months within your organization, you will inevitably take various steps during the wind down process. Some are steps of reflection while others are steps of preparation and packaging. These include:

a. Reviewing goals planned versus goals achieved
b. Paying it forward – Preparing your successors
c. Remembering insights and relationships gained throughout your career
d. Preparing for a graceful exit

Reviewing Goals Planned versus Goals Achieved

Having witnessed many of my former colleagues preparing for retirement and the triumphal exit from the workforce has been one of the highlights of my career. Watching someone who has worked very diligently for 30, 40, even 50+ years take their rightful place as a "retiree" brings feelings of happiness, joy, and even a slight bit of envy. You may have experienced some of the same emotions as you watched your colleagues log off of their work computers for the very last time, pack up the remains of their retirement cake, carefully bundle their "thanks for your service" plaques and organization-gifted ivy plants, and turn in their office keys and badges. The entire process seems very exciting and it leaves many to pull out calendars and call retirement funding companies to recalculate when their exit strategies will become reality. While the festivities of the last few days at a job are very visual and engaging for many who work alongside the latent careerist, what happens during the weeks to months preceding the retirement gala are usually handled behind closed doors by the person exiting the organization.

One of the steps that leaders take before making the transition to tossing the alarm clock is one of reflection. Many who are looking forward to retirement may also look backwards to revisit goals planned in comparison to goals achieved. For many, this process is joyous. For others, it may be disappointing. For those who have reached the goals planned in early and mid-careerist phases of their careers, revisiting that list of "*in 5 years, I will be…*" can bring about feelings of achievement and pride in a job well done. The feeling of accomplishment can only heighten the emotion that is felt during the weeks leading up to the balloons, streamers, and slide shows filled with pictures from the former days. For those who must admit to achieving or completing less than was planned during the earlier phases of the career journey, the questions become, "What happened?" "Why didn't I reach my goals as planned?" "Is it too late to make my goals reality?" "Can I still make a positive impact on my organization?"

Although the process of reviewing goals and career "to do" lists should occur throughout the career journey, the critical reviewing of goals becomes more pressing and more prevalent in the minds of those who realize they are soon leaving organizations.

For some, they feel that they need a final push to leave their mark on the workforce. Everyone wants to leave a positive influence and be thought of as someone who accomplished what they set out to do when colleagues recall their work. For those who may feel they did not accomplish all they set out to do during their working years, all is not lost. Dreams do not have to dissipate once employment ends.

Contrary to popular belief, our influence does not have to leave organizations when we do. Those who are truly influential leave their legacies with organizations by adequately preparing those who will succeed them. You can continue to be influential long after your days with a company have ended. This is accomplished by influencing others who will remain after retirees leave the organization. By engaging those who have been supporters, followers, and allies, exiting leaders have the possibility of continuing to compel others to greatness. This is a career-long process, but can also be applied in latent phases of the career journey. Those goals that can still be accomplished can be revamped and passed on to those who have the ability to complete them after you are gone. Use your influence to continue to push your dreams and goals forward by the hands of those who are like-minded and able to see the task through to completion. It is not too late to make those goals reality.

If all else fails and you decide you want to see these goals through to completion, you have the option of asking to remain as an expert for the company – not as a 9 to 5 employee, but in other aspects of freelance employment. Many retirees continue some form of relationship with leaders and influential stakeholders within organizations, whether this is in the realm of consultant, expert advisor, project lead, confidant, or simply a knowledgeable colleague who is available to discuss ideas and processes when needed. We all know someone who holds the key to finding the right answer in all situations. These are individuals that companies love to call on when a third-party expert's opinion is needed. For many retirees, this is rewarding work, yet not overwhelming. This may be the route for you if you feel you would be more inclined to see your projects to completion or your goals achieved at your hand. The opportunities are endless...if we ask.

Pay it Forward – Preparing Your Successor

One very important element of a soon-to-retire leader's responsibility is the preparation of a successor. For those who know that they want to appoint one of the current employees who has been stellar and has earned the honor of promotion, this process can begin months or years before the retiree leaves the organization. For those who may need to hire and bring a successor into the organization, there may not be as much time to acclimate the person to the role. A couple of tips can assist with this process regardless of the timeframe allotted for the transition. In a nutshell, this is called *Embracing the Successor.*

Embracing the Successor

For the new person taking on the role that you as a tenured leader are vacating, it can be a daunting process. Even if the successor has been with the organization for many years, taking on someone else's role, especially if the exiting person is held in high regard and respect, is a situation that can introduce anxiety. Coupled with the fact that some who are vacating positions may feel a bit of disdain towards the new leader and may secretly want the leader to have less impact than they did, the transition may be one that causes undue stress for the successor. While the want to withhold knowledge may be suitable for some, true leaders are willing to embrace the person coming after them because they want the organization and its leaders to succeed. The goal for the exiting leader is to ensure the successor is as well-prepared and comfortable as possible before the exit occurs. You as a leader have the option of doing what can assist the new leader in finding success early on during the transition. This process includes being **N.I.C.E.**

1. **N**ame Names – A new leader will need contact information for those who can assist with being successful. For those who are entering organizations while taking on the former leader's role, this information becomes very important to share. Be sure to give the successor names, email addresses, phone numbers and other tips for successful interactions for those who are key players and influential within organizations and your network. This can ensure a smoother transition than if the successor is left to find that information by trial and error. Also, remember to give your personal contact information in case your successor needs info on some areas you are deemed "the expert." Remember, sharing knowledge that can help others succeed does not mean we become deficient or will be viewed as subordinate. Leaders share because they want others to succeed. Withholding information that we know is critical to the success of another is not a leadership move.

2. **I**ntroduce – One of the greatest gifts that an existing leader can give a successor is the gift of introducing the new leader to influential people in the organization or business community. Doing these initial introductions is more personable than asking the new leader to "reach out to make contact." Giving this official handoff to your contacts speaks volumes of your willingness to ensure the new leader and the relationships between the organization and its stakeholders succeed. This may also assist you with becoming the go-to advisor or consultant for these stakeholders in the future because of the professionalism

and support exhibited during this interaction. This small act shows that you are not solely interested in your success, but you genuinely care about the success of the business, customers, projects, etc. This also gives the new leader an open door because of the relationships the exiting leader started for them. This is a great tool for cementing the *"you are being left in good hands"* mentality. This can yield greater respect for you as a leader.

3. Congratulate – Openly congratulate and show honor to the person who is succeeding you. For some, this may be difficult if the latent careerist is not ready to leave the organization or if the exiting careerist feels the successor is going to be more accepted than he or she was. Truth be told, if this is the feelings associated with the succession process, the exit of the former "leader" may have been well needed. Being intimidated by another is not common to true leaders. Leaders do not withhold or withdraw because someone else may get the attention we crave. Leaders will do what is necessary to ensure the success of the organization, project, or initiative. Leaders understand that this process can create buy-in for the team, other leaders within the organization, and the successor. Giving your stamp of approval gives the new leader a positive jump on the relationship building process within the organization. As my friend and esteemed editor, Eric Mitchell says, *"plus, it's just classy."*

4. Empower – Well before your last day with the organization, allow the successor to take the lead on some of the projects, meetings, and communications that you are tasked with completing. This will allow the successor to ask questions, learn from mistakes, and grow relationships while you are still present to be a confidant, preceptor, and expert in real time. This smooth transition process will be more comfortable for you, the organization, and your successor

because it will give confidence and build knowledge for the successor while they have you as an in-person backup resource.

These are easy tips to ensure successful transitions for both you and your successor, and ultimately the organization. Leaving in a disorderly fashion will potentially ruin your reputation with the company. Unfortunately, too many people exit organizations after failing to meet the mark during their last few days to months on the job. A lifetime of excellence can be overshadowed by a couple of months of lackadaisical work or inability or refusal to properly prepare the next in line. Leaders do not act in such a manner, but they ensure ease of transition for the organization and people they have served throughout their careers. Following this process will allow you to continue to shine as a leader, guide, mentor, and developer long after your time with the company. You will continue to form bonds and show yourself worthy of being called "leader" and "expert" to those who may regale your days long after you exit the organization. Also, these actions may open doors to your potential for being called upon for expert or consultant-type opportunities after your official post with the company is complete. Your legacy of leadership will be evident if these steps are followed.

Leaders' Lesson: Share Freely – Don't Hoard Vital Information

What do you wish someone would have told you at the start of your career? Do you wish you could have picked the brains of those considered experts in your organizations? Did you have someone who showed you the ins and outs of the company and offered up assistance if needed or did you encounter those who attempted to hide and hoard information because they wanted to be seen as the expert on a topic? Try to remember what you felt if you were not embraced by those you had to work with…and vow to do the opposite. Offer up assistance. Offer your time, your help, and your brain if needed. Share what you know. Share your insights. Share your successes and failures. What have you learned throughout your career? What can you share with your incoming successor that will help that leader avoid mistakes that you made? Be sure to share these insights freely and without hesitation. Be transparent. These lessons will help others succeed. This is what leaders do.

Leadership is not a competition that only one person can win. Leadership is a journey. Each one has to take a separate path to leadership. Help others coming after you be successful in reaching their personal and professional goals. Start, continue, and end your career strong. Reflect on what you accomplished and what you have to celebrate. Remember the items that must be passed on and give the next in line the tools to be successful at attaining those set goals. Do everything you can to be able to say, "I started and ended my career like a leader." Parents are often told that the goal of a parent is to ensure their children are better off and did better in life than their parents. We want those succeeding us to do better than we did. That is a very noble statement which should also apply to those who succeed us in business…if we are truly leaders.

PART II

What is Leadership (...and What It's Not)?

"A leader is one who knows the way, goes the way, and shows the way." – John C. Maxwell

There are many opinions, theories, and ideas regarding leaders and leadership. If you search for quotes regarding leadership, there are more found online than you could have imagined. There is no shortage of books regarding leadership; seminars on how to become an effective leader; and people who deem themselves a "leader" because of their positioning in organizations. While there are many who consider themselves leaders, many cannot speak to what a leader is. We first need to know what a leader is and how a leader leads in order to give a true account of those who are leaders and those who are self-chosen imposters.

Some of the most beautiful quotes on leadership (in my opinion) were compiled by Kruse (2012). While there are many quotes on the list of *Forbes 100 Best Quotes on Leadership*, some of my favorites are listed below:

> *"Where there is no vision, the people perish."* – King Solomon (Proverbs 29:18, KJV)

"A leader is best when people barely know he exists, when his work is done, his aim fulfilled, they will say: 'We did it ourselves.'" – Lao Tzu

"I must follow the people; am I not their leader?" – Benjamin Disraeli

"The first responsibility of a leader is to define reality. The last is to say thank you. In between, the leader is a servant." – Max DePree

"Leadership is the capacity to translate vision into reality." – Warren Bennis

"Before you are a leader, success is all about growing yourself. When you become a leader, success is all about growing others." – Jack Welch

"Leadership is lifting a person's vision to high sights, the raising of a person's performance to a higher standard, the building of a personality beyond its normal limitations." – Peter Drucker

"Become the kind of leader that people would follow voluntarily; even if you had no title or position." – Brian Tracy

"Leaders become great not because of their power, but because of their ability to empower others." – John Maxwell

"Average leaders raise the bar on themselves; good leaders raise the bar for others; great leaders inspire others to raise their own bar." – Orrin Woodward

"Leadership is an action, not a position." – Donald McCannon

"A leader takes people where they want to go. A great leader takes people where they don't necessarily want to go but ought to be." – Rosalynn Carter

What do all of these beautiful quotes have in common? All of the quotes give ideals related to leadership based solely on one premise: What leaders do. The quotes all show the commonality of *action* that leads and fuels leadership. I would dare say leadership is an action word. I would venture to say *leadership is a verb, not a noun*. Leaders are not leaders solely based on the ability to deliver a speech. Leaders are leaders because they can deliver results. Leaders act. Leaders help. Leaders uplift. Leaders support. In short, if you claim the title of "leader," yet do not display the actions held therein, consider revising your title.

In the next couple of chapters, we will discuss what leaders do, who leaders are, and how leaders lead.

CHAPTER 4

Are Leaders Born or Made?

"Leaders are not born or made — they are self-made." —
Steven Covey

**What do you think of the above quote? Think of
your answer as we move through this chapter.**

Have you had the pleasure of witnessing a baby being born? Have
you held the squirming child as you as the mother or father looked
on in amazement with tears in your eyes as the child cried for the
first time? Are you an aunt, uncle, grandparent, friend, coworker,
or loved one of someone who proudly sent the cutest little baby
pictures of their new addition dressed in jazzy little outfits? What
were your thoughts at that time? Did you look at the little one
and say, *"this baby is going to be someone great?"* Did you look at the
tiny little person and think, *"Wow, I can tell this one is a leader."*
Are you a parent who thought, *"My child is going to change the
world?"* Outside of the emotion that exudes from the moment
of a new little being entering the world and the well wishes and
blessings that we receive when presenting the new baby, how can
we know if a baby will be a leader at first glance? This leads into
the discussion that many leadership theorists revisit decade after
decade: *"Are leaders born or made?"*

Born Theory

As discussed at the beginning of the book, most of us had childhood dreams of becoming someone great. Some of us had delusions of grandeur at an early age that manifested in our incessant need to assure others around us that we were superheroes and superheroines in our own right. Was that simply child's play or were some of us getting a vision of what we would become in later years? Although we may not have physical capes or a giant "S" supplanted on our chests, maybe we saw ourselves doing amazing things as adults even while we were too young to accomplish those things.

Have you ever watched children playing in your home, neighborhood, or at a park? Have you noticed that many of the children were innately drawn to one child more than others? The person who was deemed the epitome of a cool playmate usually chose the games played, the areas traveled, and the slides conquered for the other little ones. Do you remember being the child who others loved to seek out on the playground or the child who was always chosen first for a team game?

Let's fast forward to high school-aged children. Think back to your days of high school. Were you the person others fought to sit next to in class? Were you the person others looked to for guidance as to what lunch items were "cool" and should be consumed? Whom did you look to when attempting to pick out wardrobes that would be acceptable in your social setting? Although many did not walk around using the word "leader" in high school, were there children who were known as the ones to emulate or befriend? Were these children "born leaders" or were they somehow taught at a very young age to display characteristics that set them apart from the crowd? While some may call this process of some children molding the ideas, thoughts, and perceptions of other children who seem to unprotestingly follow them "peer pressure" when it is noticed in child-aged circles, others call it leadership when displayed in adults.

Children in the formative years of life have not lived long enough to gain experiences deemed necessary to "make" leaders, right? Surely those experiences discussed above are not learned because most of those children have not lived long enough to learn what works and what does not. These traits and characteristics are innate for many.

In the debate of leaders being born versus made, leaders and leadership have been dissected down to atomic levels. Theorists who believe that leaders are born have operated on the notion that there are certain given markers that all leaders possess and these can be traced back to the early years of life. According to DeNeve et al (2013), leaders are born with markers that identify them as leaders. These scientists researched and studied groups of fraternal and identical twins. "The Twin Studies" identified a trait/gene component in one twin which was not consistently evident in the other twin. The researchers deduced that leadership may be associated with a specific genetic marker, rs4950, a single nucleotide polymorphism (SNP) that resides on the neuronal acetylcholine receptor gene on a chromosome. In addition, DeNeve et al (2013) found there was only a 10% correlation in leadership traits and environment shared (the womb) while other genetic components of the twins' biological makeup correlated at 24%. The science seems to back the notion that leaders are born, but born theorists also presented an added component. "Born" theorists believe that leaders have the means, but must make the choice of using their God-given birthright to exude leadership.

Have you ever encountered someone that you knew could do better than they were doing? Have you spoken to a friend, loved ones, coworkers, or employees who you know had the potential for reaching their goals because they showed that strength in the past yet they refused to do so at that moment? Did you believe those individuals were choosing to settle for "less than" instead of stepping into what was innately gifted to them? On the opposite side of this spectrum, have you witnessed someone who knew they wanted to achieve a certain goal push forward in the face of adversity? Have you had the awe-inspiring opportunity to witness a child born into despondent situations rise up to become a great leader or a sought after athlete? Many of us may know someone who was born to mothers or fathers who did not support, uplift, or encourage them. Some of us know people who were physically or mentally abused and who were told they would "never be anything or anyone." While some may have taken these words spewed in hate as a death sentence and reality, those who decided that these put downs were not law used the negativity to fuel determination in themselves. The latter realized that the fight was worth it. For those who fought to prove those who hurt them wrong, they determined to reach their goals by invoking their given talents, gifts, and the innate characteristics that ultimately led them to greatness. This is the caveat to the "born" leadership theory.

Although there may be traits, characteristics, and even genes that a person is born with that sets them apart from others, that person must <u>decide</u> to become all that they were meant to be. For leaders, this is not an external decision. It is innate within leaders to do great things. The drive and passion to be successful has to come from within. While others who may love and support us can encourage and ignite the need for us to do better for ourselves, it does not take root until we determine that we will be what we were designed and called to be. In essence, born theorists believe that without the root taking ground innately, the fruit will never bloom.

Made Theory

Many leadership theorists believe that leadership is not defined by a trait or a specific gene that is given or determined before birth. "Made" theorists believe that leadership can be taught. "Made" theorists identify sheer will and grit as being the driving forces behind the ability of a person to develop into a leader. Leadership is learned according to this theory. For example, a new graduate who may not exhibit signs of being someone who may ultimately lead the company to greatness may benefit from a senior executive taking her and molding her into a phenomenal leader. The executive may identify traits or abilities in the new graduate saleswoman that may, if nurtured and developed, benefit the individual as well as the company. The executive takes the time and effort to develop the new graduate and watches this individual grow into someone who may be considered for a lead role within the company in future years. This is "made" theory at work.

"Made" theorists believe that we can develop anyone who is willing to be developed into an effective leader. The premise is that we can train individuals to be leaders, just as we can train physicians to understand the intricacies of the human body and educators to teach. In other words, someone who wants to be a leader can surround himself with those who are seen as leaders and can emulate the behaviors and actions of those he admires. He can become a leader simply by learning and doing the work to transform himself into a leader. "Made" theorists believe that we can develop someone to lead others to greatness. The adage, "birds of a feather flock together" may be a good depiction of "made" theories and what they state.

There are many forms of "made" theory that have surfaced over the past decades. Here are a few of the many theories related to "made" theory, all of which can be learned according to those who believe leaders are "made":

1. **Behavioral Theory** states that leadership behaviors can be mimicked by others simply by watching and acting as the leader does. Leaders decide what characteristics or behaviors they want to imitate and what behaviors they do not.

2. **Contingency Theory** is based on the context of success or failure. The efficiency of a leader is solely based on the outcomes that result from the behaviors and actions taken.

3. **Situational Theory** states that the leader changes leadership styles based on the situation. In other words, certain leaders may be better suited to navigate certain situations because they can evolve to handle different situations.

4. **Relationship Theory** stated leaders are focused on interactions with others or building relationships with followers to produce positive results. This type of leadership is beneficial to an organization because of the ongoing development and return-on-investment that results from the forged relationships. An example would be a manager who mentors and uplifts her employees. The goal is to create buy-in from those being led. The result will be more leaders who can assist the company in reaching its goals.

5. **Participative Theory** states that leaders who involve their teams in decision making processes create more devotion and dedication-prone environments. This theory is often called democratic leadership and allows the leader to create buy-in to make those being led stakeholders in the success or failure of a process or idea. This allows shared control to be given to the team as opposed to the leader making all decisions.

(Western Governor's University, 2020).

All of these theories have one thing in common: The belief that we all have the ability to choose to grow and develop into leaders as opposed to being born as leaders. "Made" theorists may differ on the type of leader or the various leadership characteristics that dictate a leader's being, but the idea that anyone can develop into a leader if given the opportunity and means to do so is evident across all "made" theories.

So, which is the correct side of the debate? Are leaders born or made? Are we to define leadership as one or the other or do components of both sides of this debate exist in all leaders? Can there be a middle ground for both born and made theories that presents a third option for understanding leadership and its origins and make up? Enter Natural Born Leader (NBL) Theory.

The 3rd Option: Natural Born Leader (NBL) Theory

In 2019, Haraida and Blass did research on both the made and born theories and theorists. They identified characteristics of both theories that are prevalent in true leaders. While this theory dictates that leaders are born, the theorists believe that everyone is born a leader. The distinction of "leader" is not limited to one set of individuals born with certain chromosomes or genes. Leaders are not solely made by watching, listening, and emulating the behaviors of others. Leadership is a combination of both of these aspects of the previous two theories.

Haraida and Blass (2019) studied leaders in in the sports realm. Those who engaged in competitive sports (whether as coach, player, or an alternate position) showed innate abilities to lead others to reach goals of the team. What was discovered was that some people are true leaders who focus on growing others, supporting others, leading others, and reaching the goals of the masses while others were able to imitate signs of artificial leadership to reach their purposes. For example, Nelson Mandela, Mother Teresa, and Mohatma Gandhi are identified by Haraida and Blass (2019) as true leaders. They fought for the greater good of the masses with little regard for how they would be treated or mistreated as a result of the fight. These leaders put themselves on the line to ensure the wellbeing of those who were in need of leadership, support, and an ally. In contrast, Haraida and Blass (2019) used the examples of Mussolini, Hitler, and Donald Trump as individuals who may be called "leaders" because of the number of people who believed in their actions and style. These individuals were cited as being concerned with reaching their goals or getting what they needed, but the wellbeing of the whole was not a priority. While some can imitate "leaders," taking a closer look at how these individuals interact with others and what and whom they deemed important allows us to see that the greater good may not have been at the center of many of the decisions these pseudo-leaders made.

NBL Theory separates leaders from imitations of leadership. This theory combines attributes of both "born" and "made" theories into one incorporated theory. The most important takeaway is the distinction between true leaders and pseudo-leaders. While some may pretend to be leaders and pretend to emulate others to get what they desire, true leaders are committed to the process of fighting for the greater good. While NBL Theory is a new theory based on the history of theories past, this theory of leadership may be one that is included in coaching theories in future years.

Leaders' Lesson: Born, Made, or NBL Theory - What Do You Think?

While NBL Theory is a compilation of the two elder theories related to the origins of leaders and leadership, some may argue that NBL theory reiterates that leaders have innate characteristics that, when invoked, allows someone who may not have been seen as a "leader" to begin showing those attributes. The traits were always present, but had to be awakened in order for the leader to respond as such.

What lessons can we gain from the three theories related to the origins of leadership? Think of these questions as you reflect on what you felt prior to this chapter and how those ideas of the origins of leadership may have changed as you read through the content.

1. Regardless of what side of the debate you believe was accurate prior to now, do you feel that elements of both "born" and "made" leadership theories are accurate? Please explain.
2. Think back to your own experiences as a child then your experiences as an adult. Were there signs of leadership that were apparent in your childhood but were not invoked until later in life? Are there some traits that you feel have not been activated as of yet?
3. Reflect on the experiences of leaders in your realm. Were they all leaders when you encountered them or were they developed, grown, and cultivated into leaders at your hand or with the help of others?

CHAPTER 5

Defining and De-Mything
Manager/Boss versus Leader

*"People ask the difference between the leader and a boss.
The leader leads, the boss drives."* – Theodore Roosevelt

Have you had the experience of walking into a conference room, looking around the room, and identifying maybe one or two people who you admire for their ability to rally the team to do what is needed to accomplish a task? Did you feel honored to be collaborating with such amazing individuals who unknowingly set the bar much higher for all who encountered them? Have you glanced around the same room and had your eyes land on a handful of individuals who were infamously known as dictators or devoid of the characteristics of those identified as someone to emulate by those within your company? Have you asked the question, "Whom did he know to get that position" after witnessing a man openly ridicule a member of his team or set goals that he did not assist in reaching while constantly belittling his "subordinates?" Have you ever found yourself wondering, "How did she end up in this position" after repeatedly being exposed to a particular woman's inappropriate behaviors, negative attitude, sloth–like demeanor, "me first" outlook, and seeming inability to foster positive relationships with those within her employ? Lastly, did you witness the chair of the committee or organizer of the meeting walk into the room and address all in attendance as "leaders?" Many of us have experienced this mind-boggling event at some point during our careers. How and why would someone deem all of those present, including those we know were not worthy of such accolades "leaders?" What just happened?

Throughout my career, I experienced the phenomenon of people around me being called "leaders" regardless of their inappropriate behaviors, menacing characteristics, limited or absent business acumen, and negative traits that dictated otherwise. As an early careerist, I often bought into the unstated rule that automatically tied management level employees to the term "leadership" because this was the expectation within organizations. It seemed appropriate that those who were in higher level positions were seen as leaders because they had titles that made one *assume* they were capable of leading the masses. After a few years of witnessing those whose behaviors did not invoke feelings of admiration, respect, trust, or adulation being repeatedly and incessantly labeled as "leaders," I began pondering the notion of leadership and how it relates to management. I wondered why certain individuals were called "leaders" when they did not display characteristics that were common in those others within the organization who were esteemed as true leaders. I began considering the possibility of leadership and management not being synonymous terms, against what I had been taught earlier in my career. I started to see leadership and management for what those terms were meant to relay.

If your experience has been similar to mine and you have witnessed the terms leader and manager or boss being used synonymously, did you buy into the notion that was being sold? Do you believe leadership and management are one in the same? Should an individual be automatically considered a leader simply because of the job or position that person holds or are there characteristics, behaviors, traits, and motives that define leaders and set them apart from other individuals? To gain a better understanding of these terms, we must first define and take a deeper dive into the concepts of leadership and management.

Manager/Boss Defined

The term "manager" or "boss" is used to identify an individual who has been given a human resources- or Office of Talent Management-appointed position within an organization. This terminology is used when an individual is given governing or oversight power over another individual or groups of individuals within a company. The manager or boss is the designated entity that a group of employees are accountable to according to the hierarchical or organizational chart of the business. The manager or boss has a defined set of job functions, duties, and expectations that have been designed to promote the outcomes of the business. This includes HR-designated duties, including but not limited to interviewing, hiring, terminations, progressive discipline (also called corrective action), ensuring staffing and payroll is appropriately completed, answering complaints of customers, interacting with stakeholders, attending meetings, assisting with developing strategies that will propel the business unit and organization forward, etc. The manager or boss carries out the general HR functions of the organization, but on a localized level. Although localized, the effects of the manager's locus of control are felt at higher organizational levels.

According to the University of California at Berkeley (2021),

> "… a manager is responsible for making significant decisions on what the unit does: its purpose, functions and role, and for making commitments and decisions that require the expenditure of significant unit resources. Managers have a significant, external focus (to the world outside the unit…" (para 1).

A manager's ultimate goal is to achieve high performance from its unit. The manager's job expectations are to ensure this goal is met. The manager is a strong advocate and ally of the executive and administrative teams and represents those executives on a smaller, more intimate level than can be reached by those in higher positions. For example, a chief officer is accountable and responsible for the overall functioning and effectiveness of an organization regardless of the size of that organization. It is not feasible for the chief officer to oversee the daily operations of each subset of employees, units, and policies for each department, especially within larger organizations. It would be impossible for the chief officer to manage every detail of the organization, interact with every employee, and pioneer the planning, implementation, and revision of every goal set in each department without becoming less effective and experiencing expedited burnout. For this reason, the use of supervisors, managers, directors, and others who can act as intermediaries between the chiefs and the frontline employees is necessary to ensure the minute details of each subset or group within the organization are effectively managed. While the chief officer retains overall responsibility and oversight of the full organization, each subgroup is managed by another employee. This off-loading process allows the chief officer to focus on more pressing and global initiatives that are then passed down to those who can implement and oversee the details of the processes once given to the frontline workers.

While managers or bosses have direct reports (or employees who report directly to their job role), they are also direct reports to other roles within organizations. Managers may report to senior managers, directors, executive vice presidents, or to chief-level employees. This reporting structure causes the level of accountability and responsibility to move upward as tiers of the hierarchy move towards the chief or top level within the organization. In other words, the lower the level of the position, the closer the span of control on the frontline employees and details of individual processes. The higher the level of the position equates to more global accountability and reporting mass.

Management roles are highly results-driven. One of the defining factors in declaring a manager effective is to review the results and outcomes of the business unit over which the manager has oversight. The use of data collection and analysis tools guide the organization's upper management officers in deciding the efficacy of processes, policies, and even management on business units. For organizations that rely heavily on customer service input to drive improvements and new initiatives, feedback from customers may dictate what changes need to be instituted by managers. These changes may be handed down as mandates from higher level officers or may be left to managers to invoke. Depending on the organization and the importance of the data, officers of the organization may move to replace or remove the manager who is deemed ineffective and replace that manager with promising prospects who may be better prepared to deliver on reaching the organization's goals. With so much at stake, managers are often driven to do whatever is necessary to reach their set goals. This becomes the top priority for many in manager or boss positions and often takes more precedence over team building, employee support, and developing others. Job security and organizational goal attainment become the areas of most concern for managers and bosses, thus managers may focus all energy and talent into these initiatives.

Leaders

In contrast to managers, leaders may or may not hold official officer positions of power or appointment within organizations. Leadership does not have to be an official appointment that coincides with a hierarchical structure within an organization. Leaders may be officially or unofficially given power. This power may be absolute (given by authority of another in an appointed position) or perceived (respected and seen as influential by others). Simply put, leaders do not have to be HR-appointed officers within organizations, but may be those who can, by using unofficial power, influence peers, friends, and others to improve themselves and promote positive outcomes within their organizations and professional and personal circles. Leaders may be frontline workers, management level employees, or others in our community who are sought out to help bring about change and empowerment for those in need. While the power that accompanies someone who is deemed a leader may not be attached to an official title or office, that power may have a very deep impact on those within their circles.

Think back to the earlier discussion of children on the playground deciding whom to follow or high school aged children who are given the ability to decide what is "cool" and what is not. While we may believe these instances may seem to be isolated to summer hangouts situations or neighborhood playground sporting event scenarios, those who work or reside in settings where we interact with children have felt the far reach of the leaders of the pack and their influence on the whole.

Years ago, I threw a weekend long birthday party for my niece, Christyan, who was entering her teen years. I remember planning and paying for two days of fun activities that I assumed girls of age 12 and 13 would enjoy. I reserved a day of fun at a local gaming events arcade. My niece's friends would be able to take part in bowling, table tennis, pool, various arcade games, laser tag, obstacle course competitions, etc. The best feature was the never-ending pizza and birthday cake that the girls could enjoy during the event. Everyone enjoyed the events at the venue. As we left the entertainment company's parking lot, everyone was excited and super-hyper about the party and what was next to come. We piled into our cars to head home. There were two cars transporting the girls to my home – one driven by Chris's mom and my sister, Carmel, and the other load of girls were driven home in my car. On the way home, I announced the plans for the evening to the group of young girls who were riding in my car pool. There was a consensus of excitement throughout my car as I explained what we would do that evening. We rode home in an environment of energy and pre-teen giggles as we prepared for a fun evening.

That night, after everyone showered and donned pajamas, we gathered in the living room. When I told the rest of the group (those riding in the second car) the planned events for that evening, I noticed half of the group was very excited to participate in the festivities while the other half did not seem very interested. I watched as those who were once very excited about the plans they learned of earlier during the ride home suddenly look to others in the group to feel out if participating would be the "in" thing to do. At the end of this phenomenon, the consensus was that the girls did not want to do planned events because that was "young," but they would rather watch episodes of the latest popular teen movie to see a guy they all agreed was "the hottest-thing-walking" turn people into vampires. I endured hours of giggles and snickers at a movie that I wanted to fall asleep on, but I continued to be shocked and stumped at the very abrupt turn of the evening's events at the hands of one or two people out of 10 who were invited for the sleep over. What happened?

As I chatted and laughed with my sisters, Carmel and Sharen, about this incident, I had to take a moment to think of what could have caused my plans to go awry. I later learned that the incident above had a simple explanation: Those who were considered the "it-girls" in the group dictated what was acceptable for the group and what was not. Strangely enough, all of this took place without words, but with the use of simple looks from the pre-teen girls. Those "that's not cool" looks were effective enough to change the outlook of the whole group, even for those who initially agreed that my plans were "so awesome." This phenomenon may be labeled "peer pressure" or "the cool crew effect" in younger years, but it is also very present in the adult world (although on a different level and often under different circumstances). The label changes to "leadership" when influence is used to affect someone's life or to promote positive outcomes for those in the workplace, human circles, or communities.

Leaders are different from managers. Leaders focus more on people than on processes. Leaders may not be accountable to an entity or higher officer to ensure goals of a project or a policy are correctly implemented. Leaders may or may not have HR-appointed control over people's behaviors or performance. In essence, leaders can be those working on the same level as those who respect them. The relationship may not be hierarchical, but may be unofficial and unaffected by deadlines and mandates handed down by executive-level officers. Leaders can influence the influential even if the leader is in a position lower than their manager or boss. While each leader cannot and will not be given a position of official control, leaders do affect the outcomes of the group to which they belong.

Revisiting the slumber party scenario, I was the adult in the house, but the influential pre-teen girls who others looked up to were clearly the unofficial leaders of the group. While I had the power to overrule what was silently decided, the girls would have been disengaged and maybe even disgruntled if forced to do what everyone suddenly agreed was not fun. The same is true with adult leaders. Many of us have experienced the ability of one person to steer the crowd in the necessary direction to ensure engagement is maintained or initiatives are embraced. Regardless of whether that person had official or unofficial power, the group often relates to and supports that person who is seen as the leader. This is what leadership is: *The ability to positively influence other individuals to meet the needs of the whole.*

Behaviors and Characteristics Differences –
Manager/Boss vs. Leader

> *"Management is doing things right; leadership is doing the right things."* – Peter F. Drucker

How do those identified as "leaders" show up to those around them? What methods do these individuals use that assists others with naming them "leaders?" There are some management-level employees who are correctly identified as leaders while others are incorrectly termed "leaders" secondary to the positions they hold and regardless of their behaviors or ability to lead. This synonymous use of the term "leader" is an injustice and disservice by those who freely use this word to describe those who are not worthy of the distinction. This is a common problem seen throughout most organizations. There must be a distinction made between the two terms which identify those who are leaders versus those who are hired and appointed management-level employees.

While the definitions of leader are vast and many, there are definite characteristics and behaviors that are apparent in true leaders. There are also ideals, behaviors, and characteristics that are observed in those who are in management but are not leaders. It is important to point out that although some managers may be leaders and some leaders may hold official positions of management, these two terms are not one in the same.

In table 5.1, some identifying behaviors of leaders and managers are displayed. As you review this list, you will be able to add more terms based on your experiences with or as a leader. Think back to those true leaders you have encountered throughout your career. What are some of the behaviors, characteristics, and traits that these individuals exhibited?

Table 5.1 – Leaders Behaviors vs. Manager/Boss Behaviors

Leader Behaviors	Manager/Boss Behaviors
Highly Transformational	Routinely Transactional
Leads	Dictates
Earns respect based on merit	Demands "respect" based on position
Team-centric approach	Task-centric approach
Asks for input from team	Dictates necessary actions
Uses inspiration and empathy	Uses fear and intimidation
Coaches employees to meet goals	Micromanages to meet goals
Joins in to help	Looks on and gives orders
Gives praise and accolades	Takes credit
Verbiage: Team, group, "us"	Verbiage: Employees, subordinates, "you"

TRImani Consulting, LLC (2021)

Reviewing the list above may have brought back moments of adoration as well as memories of despair and disappointment in some we thought would lead us. The list above can invoke feelings of passion, drive, and commitment, or reminders of unreachable goals, unrealistic deadlines, and threat-laced pushes to "get it done" without the prospect of attempting to question the implementer. While leaders uplift, bosses beat down. Leaders often take the blame pointed at their team while bosses give blame to disperse the blame handed down to them. While leaders say, "let's go," bosses often say "go."

Why is there a vast difference between the actions and behaviors of some and the behaviors of others? Do these behaviors and how we interact with others stem from innate characteristics that leaders have in their arsenals? Why do some act inappropriately and not in line with how they should respond to those around them?

Thinking back to the chapter on the debate viewpoints of leaders being either born or made, we identified three potential aspects to this debate. Those who say leaders are born with certain traits or characteristics; those who believe anyone can become a great leader if they are exposed to the correct people and situations; and those who believe elements of both sides of the argument are true and leaders can use their innate abilities to inspire those around them. All three of these theories have one thing in common: All three agree that leaders exhibit certain behaviors, characteristics, and traits that, when invoked and instituted, have the potential to create amazing results.

If we took a survey on the attributes of leaders, we would notice some of the same words used to describe characteristics of leaders and what many agree denotes leadership. As a certified leadership and executive coach, I often ask my clients, "what characteristics do you feel are most important for leaders to exhibit?" No matter how many times I ask the question, some of the same answers are repeatedly identified and displayed in word cloud results. The list below is a compilation of some of the descriptive words, characteristics, and attributes used to describe leaders from past clients and audiences.

Table 5.2 – Identified Attributes/Attitudes of Leaders

Identified Attributes/attitudes of Leaders:

Uplifting	Have my back
Supportive	Welcoming
Guiding	Open
Team-success oriented	Great mentor
Willing to foster growth through learning	Cheerleader
Caring	Positive
Nurturing	Inspiring
Accessible	Innovative
Trustworthy	Aspirational
Dependable	Passionate
Expert, but not belittling	Compassionate
Dedicated	Motivating
Willing to help out	Encouraging
Coach	Respectful
Great communicator	Sets good example

TRImani Consulting, LLC (2021)

This is by no means an exhaustive list of leader attributes and what we expect from leaders. You may have a plethora of other words that you can add to this list. One common theme is presented in many of the words listed: *Action*. Leadership is about action. It bears repeating that leadership is a verb, not a noun. It is not a title that can be taken without some form of work being instituted on the part of the taker. The idea of leadership is only as strong as the actions of its owner.

Have you witnessed someone who was deemed a leader when first introduced to you transition into someone that caused that individual to begin losing that respect and the leadership accolade as time progressed? The behaviors and motives of that individual may have changed as new challenges presented. Did the person once thought of as a "leader" suddenly or eventually become seen as a "dictator" or "boss?" What occurred? Did the attributes and traits that person once displayed decide to take up residence elsewhere to make room for someone who showed the opposite characteristics or can some imitate the characteristics and traits of leaders to reach their own causes or goals? Take for example those who were mentioned in the defining of Natural Born Leaders (NBL) Theory (Haraida & Blass, 2019) in chapter 2. At first glance, many would consider those mentioned as leaders because of their ability to transform the opinions and thinking of the masses. People like Hitler, Mussolini, and Donald Trump were able to bring about changes that may not have been favorable by using influence and power to overshadow common sense in others. These individuals were able to mimic what some felt were attributes of leaders until a closer look was taken. These individuals were able to abruptly halt what some were thinking and what some believed to be true to propel their own agendas forward. While this may be influence or power, these individuals did not display characteristics of leaders according to Haraida & Blass (2019). If we are honest, regardless of our opinions of these individuals, we can agree that these displays were more appropriate to the boss or dictator characteristics displayed in previous tables and figures. Would these behaviors be appropriate in your workplace or would such behaviors be quickly addressed if you displayed them? Would we tolerate someone we work with behaving in the same manner?

Back to those we once thought of as leaders who eventually proved us wrong. Were their seemingly innate leadership qualities now changed to boss or management-type displays of power and influence or were we temporarily blinded to what was really there all along? I would venture to say that those who are leaders continue to be leaders. Leadership transcends lifetimes. We do not begin being leaders only to end up being terroristic or malicious to others because of the belief that our agendas are most important. Leaders do not forfeit the well-being and success of the whole to promote and uplift self. While those who are yielding power that comes with position may for a short time pose as leaders, their true attributes and natures always present. We must ensure these two concepts do not fall into the realm of mistaken identity and blurred lines. Be vigilant in mentally identifying imposters. This will allow you to protect yourself and your well-being when presented with those individuals.

Now that we have discussed what a manager/boss is and what a leader is, it is imperative to reiterate that these two terms are not identical but may overlap in some areas. Great leaders can be in positions of management, but this is not always the case. Those working diligently on our frontlines and behind the scenes as campaign personnel known for selflessly cheering us on can be leaders that uplift and support us. Many we manage can be seen as leaders to us and vice versa. Give more thought and contemplation to the leaders you work with each day. Make it a point to thank those people for who they are, what they stand for, and what they display that positively affects the outcomes of your business and your communities.

Effects of Leaders on Followers

We all know amazing management level employees who are strong leaders within our organizations. We know that there are those who stand out among the group of managers or bosses we have encountered throughout our years who are deserving of the title "leader." We also know some who may never be in positions of management, yet these individuals invoke the same feelings of support, encouragement, and motivation that some leaders in management positions present. The distinction between management/boss and leader is the positive impact (or lack thereof) that those individuals have on those around them.

The greatest effect felt in the workplace and in our communities is the effect leaders have on their followers and those they are entrusted to lead. Leaders not only lead by example, but they ultimately cause the outlook and behaviors of those around them to change as well. This is one of the distinguishing attributes of leaders. Leaders can lead others to greatness, even when they do not realize the impact they have on those watching them. While we may not realize it and it may not be stated repeatedly as we go about our daily duties, we have an impact on those who encounter us. There are many around us who look to us as unofficial mentors and leaders. This is what leaders do. Leaders transform. The telltale sign of a leader is the impact of that person on those they encounter. Someone who openly deems themselves a leader, yet does not invoke changes for better in those around them is misguided and ill-suited for their self-given title. Leaders are followed, respected, emulated, and imitated by those whose lives they have changed and by those who are empowered and encouraged in their presence.

Leaders' Lesson: Are You Honoring Those Who Led You?

Think on these questions as we complete this chapter on leadership versus management.

1. What made those individuals who shaped your career stand out in your mind as leaders?
2. What did those individuals say or do to make you remember their leadership with fondness and admiration?
3. How did that person make you feel about the tasks at hand?
4. Are you emulating what was felt when you encountered the great leaders you recalled? If not, what can you do to pay homage to the great example the leaders in your life have set?

PART III

Self-leadership – Developing Yourself to Develop Others

"Learning is not a one-time event or periodic luxury. Great leaders in great companies recognize that the ability to constantly learn, innovate, and improve is vital to their success." – Amy Edmondson

Growth is vital to living beings. When we cease growing, we cease living. This is true from the cellular level to the noticeably physical level of any being. Hair, fingernails, muscles, skin, and other parts of our bodies regenerate and grow according to the nutrients and care given by the owner. Just as plants grow by using elements of the environment to nourish and sustain, we grow by using elements around us. For leaders, this includes knowledge gained from lived experiences, learning processes, and supportive mechanisms. Leaders use these elements to become sustainable in business and in life. While the goal of leaders is to grow more leaders, the priority is to ensure the leader's self-development. An undeveloped or underdeveloped seed cannot produce other plants. A child cannot successfully and effectively raise another child. The child must rely on others who have travailed life and learned lessons of sustainability along the way. This is true of leaders as well. Before we can assist others in developing, we must develop ourselves.

As you read through this section of the book, consider how important your self-development is to you and those around you. Consider ways to ensure you are well-developed for the tasks you must complete as a leader, including being well-suited to develop others.

CHAPTER 6

Understanding Your Leadership Style

What is a leadership style?

Depending on who is asked, defined leadership styles will differ based on the period that this concept was learned by that individual. For others, it depends on the concepts their organizations promote. For some, leadership styles are limited to a few choices: Laissez-faire, Authoritative, and Authoritarian. To others, leadership styles include terms such as Transformational, Transactional, Participative, Delegative, etc. Some thought leaders identify three leadership styles. Others identify six, while others identify seven or more leadership styles. There is no shortage of theories and theorists related to leadership styles...and confusion related to which is most appropriate and acceptable for different audiences.

Have you had the experience of being asked "what's your leadership style" during an interview process? Regardless of context, this question always invokes a moment of contemplation. Whether the question is posed by someone leading an interview for a job to which you are applying or if the source of the question is a potential hire that you are interviewing for your company, the answer is usually compiled with some sort of rambling and seeking for the correct words to define who we are, what we do, and what we support. Some of us may laugh when thinking back to situations where we fumbled around adjectives for 2 minutes while attempting to find the right words to appropriately portray who we are as leaders. Others may have rehearsed an answer and are able to recall it at a moment's notice to ensure they come across as well-identified and self-actualized when the question is posed. Strangely enough, some of our answers may change given the audience or the objective of the assignment to be had. The focus may switch to fitting into the group or meeting the favor of the hiring person seeking the "ideal candidate."

Although this is a question that is usually asked in any interview or meeting where we are being considered for a position where others will be entrusted to the role in question, the answer usually evades us for a moment. Why is that? Could it be because we succumb to the styles others dictate are currently definitive of leadership? Are we, in the midst of our seeking, attempting to find the "right answer" for the times in which the question is asked? While we may have muttered off "democratic" as our leadership style when asked 10 years ago, do we now mentally search for the most up-to-date definition of leadership and the most popular leadership style before settling on "transformational?" While the terms and adjectives related to leadership styles may change with the times, if we have a constant, simple definition of "leadership style," we should be able to describe who we are and how we show up, not by our own volition, but by the input we receive from others.

The Self-proclaimed (Sometimes False) Leadership Style

Simply put, one's leadership style defines how a person acts, interacts, and reacts to any work, challenges that arise related to that work, and the people carrying out the work. A constant misconception is that leadership style is dictated by subjective input. On the contrary, leadership style is dictated by those being led. While those leading may state, "I'm democratic," the person's actual style is identified by those who may or may not agree. If those on the team or those in the group that is subjected to an individual are stating, "her style is more authoritative than democratic," this is probably true because leadership is highly objective, not subjective. Although many call themselves "leader," there may or may not be consensus from those who interact closely with (and must endure being around) some self-proclaimed leaders. The question for each of us should become, "what is my leadership style based on input and feedback from those I am blessed to lead?" To present this question and the ultimate reflections that will result from it, you must have the confidence and openness to take constructive criticism, input, and tips from people around you who are comfortable being open and candid with you.

There are many who feel that one's leadership style may be confined to one word or another. This is a subject that is presented in many workplace forums and conference room discussions. In most organizational leadership seminars, webinars, or conferences, there is usually some form of presentation on leadership style and what style is appropriate for that period of time. How many conferences have you attended where you were asked to identify your "leadership style?" No matter how many times I witness this process, it never ceases to amaze me when I watch people scurry to corners that identify various styles of leadership. When asked to identify which of the 6+ (depending on the author of the concept) leadership styles the attendees identify with, there is a plethora of people who automatically seeks out the group titled, "transformational." Very few stand in the circle related to "transactional," "autocratic," bureaucratic," "laissez-faire," etc. I would venture to say that this is a misrepresentation.

Think back to leadership seminars you have attended. Have you witnessed people who were highly autocratic or intentionally bureaucratic join the transformational group only to be given stares of "you don't belong here" by those who knew better? Have you tried to hold back your reaction as you watched self-proclaimed "leaders" who you know were consistently ineffective, backstabbing, demanding, or belittling to their team speak the words, "I'm a democratic leader" when the presenter asked participants to present their self-chosen leadership style? Is it because these individuals are not self-aware or is it because they followed what was deemed the "best" or most effective style or one that would not be ridiculed? Why was there little regard to how those individuals really show up to their teams and peers?

Just as children of middle and high school years navigate to what's popular, this occurs in adult circles as well. There are some forms or styles of leadership that are more acceptable than others. This leads people to identify with those styles of leadership while falsely and often inappropriately distancing themselves from others.

Leaders must understand and embrace who they are and use this to their advantage. The style of a leader is not dictated by the social norms or pressures related to what is "best" or "most effective," but is directly related to the qualities, values, and actions of the leader as perceived by the follower. It is safe to say that a leader's best and most accurate indicator of leadership effectiveness and leadership style depends on the input of those around the leader.

With that said, what's the most appropriate leadership style? Is there one leadership style that fits all circumstances and needs of a team? Would someone who is democratic benefit an organization when strict deadlines are handed down and executives do not embrace input on a project that could affect the longevity of the company? Would someone who is deemed authoritarian in style be appropriate to lead in times when maintaining employee engagement are of optimal importance? While some of these characteristics of each leadership style may not be appropriate at all times, there are times when some of each style's traits may be appropriate to yield the intended results of the team or organization.

Target Leadership Style: Flexible

To be effective, leaders must first understand themselves and how they function. Secondly, leaders must embrace themselves for who they are. Leaders who are prone to select one leadership style that they are *told* is more effective than another are usually not doing themselves justice. How many of the leaders within any organization are solely democratic or solely transformational? The choosing of one specific leadership style as the gold standard and constant style of any leader is to invoke a robotic leadership mentality without respect for differing situations, persons, and circumstances. Once again, we must make a distinction at this point to ensure clarity. This type of presentation may be indicative of managers/bosses, but not leaders. This phenomenon is akin to one stating he is always disgruntled or consistently in a state of peace. This is unrealistic in the realm of human beings. Human beings have different emotions and a broad spectrum of reactions to various situations that we encounter. Stating we react one way to every situation, whether good or unfavorable, is a misrepresentation of our character. The same is true for leaders.

You probably can picture various individuals you have encountered throughout your career who were constantly autocratic, bureaucratic, or authoritarian without flexibility. If all situations, encounters, and meetings ended with one person controlling each aspect of what was discussed and decided without respect for the input of others or the creation of consensus among the group, that person may have held a position of manager or boss, but does not exhibit the capabilities of a leader. This personality type may work for single-celled organisms, but thinking, capable, intelligent adults work best and yield more effective results when they are included in the processes surrounding their work when feasible. You may also know someone who is constantly laissez-faire or democratic in style. These characteristics may work in some situations, but not in others. Practicing solely one way without the ability or want to flex according to the situation is not conducive to the human experience.

Leaders are flexible. Styles can and should change according to the situation. While leaders may sometimes be democratic and may often promote input and interaction with others to gather input from the masses, those same leaders may be forced to change to a more transactional or authoritarian style to ensure the team carries out processes in a timely and efficient manner. When the bottom line is at risk and timelines are tight (e.g., when there is a threat of reduction in force if timed goals are not met or if a key shareholder is expected to visit to follow up on a mandatory initiative that was instituted earlier that week), leaders may not have time to gather individuals for brainstorming meetings and to see how everyone feels about the mandates. Having been in healthcare for a couple of decades, I experienced the authoritarian leadership style present during times of regulatory accreditation surveys. Leaders who were otherwise democratic or transformational suddenly needed to quickly switch to a more "take charge" leadership style to get mandates and tasks updated and instituted quickly. The ability of the leader to call meetings with all staff and get input and feedback on the chiefs' mandates for quick change was not warranted. The changes had to be instituted and processes had to be put in place to ensure the goals were met in an expedited manner and without much question or pushback by the team. The offering of an incentive at the time of completion (e.g., a bonus or pizza party) may have sometimes assisted with reaching the goals as stated, but the offering of suggestions related to the mandatory tasks was not solicited in such instances. The leader's style had to change to meet the urgent needs of the organization.

This quick change process is also seen with leaders who interact with individual employees. Just as children born to the same household have distinct characteristics and personalities that parents must learn to navigate in order to create buy in (and to stay sane), members of teams have different personalities. Each person is different and may respond to input, support, and suggestions in a different manner. What works for one person may not work for others. For example, there are some who are easily motivated and quick to buy into whatever is needed to advance the organization. Others may need a little prompting or support to do so. Some may not respond to the niceties that motivate others. These individuals may respond to defined, succinct, and very directive input from the leader. Leaders must be able to change styles to effectively reach those in the intended audience.

It is safe to say that a good target style for leaders is "**flexible**." Leaders must flex their styles to meet the situation and needs of the team or process being addressed. This is a principle of life as well as leadership. Many have learned that we cannot lead a group of Millennials in the same manner that we lead those who belong to the generations of Baby Boomers and Gen X. While one group is highly loyal to the organization and would opt to work around difficult managers, policies, and the job hey hold, the other group may focus on what can benefit individuals instead of the organization. The goals, beliefs, attitudes, and outlooks of different generations may differ. What is easily grasped for some may not be grasped for other groups.

One of the most difficult transitions for healthcare organizations was the transition from paper charting to the electronic medical record. Healthcare professionals who were not exposed to the Internet or online modalities during their degree programs suddenly had to switch to solely online documentation. Those nurses and providers who were Baby

Boomers found some difficulty during the transition while those in Gen X and Millennial generations were able to transition with much less opposition. Some who were not willing to or able to accommodate the new modality opted to leave organizations or move to organizations where computer charting had not yet been instituted. Others decided to take Internet and Computer Basics courses or work diligently to learn the new computerized charting processes. In this world, flexibility is required. If one is not able to be flexible, exit may be inevitable.

Imagine you are traveling to Japan to act as the headlining speaker for a conference on effective leadership. You decide that you are going to present the entire presentation in English because that is the language you speak. Without ensuring you can flex your presentation to meet the needs, accepted demeanor, and cultural colloquialisms of the audience, you deliver your speech without the use of a translator and official orator who is well-versed in the culture of your audience. When asked if a translator could be of assistance to ensure your audience understands what is being relayed, you refuse to use the more effective way of communicating to that audience. How effective would your speech on "effectiveness" be if you are not able to reach your audience? How effective is your leadership if the style you embrace and display does not meet the needs of the team or initiative?

Another example: Your organization's board tells you that it is imperative to get a go-live progress report to them before close of business on a same-day implemented initiative for your sales team. Your "democratic" style of leadership leads you to spend much of the day pulling together meetings with most of your departments and salespeople to ensure everyone is onboard and all input has been received before implementing the process. The planning for and conducting meetings with various departments take up most of the time needed to ensure successful implementation of the new mandate; therefore, the board's goal was not met. What would be the outcome? Would the board understand that you are a democratic leader and had to seek the input of the frontline before moving forward? If so, please let me know what organization you work for because I would love to work there. In most cases, your actions would result in some form of untoward discipline.

Flexibility for leaders is imperative to ensure success. Leaders cannot be confined to one distinct and very separate style and be considered effective. As situations, people, attitudes, times, and the world around us change, we must flex our styles to promote success in the environment in which we exist. Using a flexible leadership style allows the organism to align with the goals and people of the organization to promote better outcomes for all stakeholders.

Leaders' Lesson: Current vs. Targeted Leadership Style

To correctly identify your leadership style, uncomfortable action may have to be taken. This may present revelations regarding your self-perceived versus actual leadership style and abilities. While this process may be uncomfortable at first, it may help you better understand who you are and where you are in your leadership journey and can ultimately assist with reaching future leadership goals. This process will assist you with getting a clear depiction of where you are versus what you have to do to get where you wish to be as a leader.

Ask the following questions and seek out honest, candid answers from those who work alongside you:

1. What is your stated leadership style?
2. If your peers, teammates, or those you lead are asked to define your leadership style, how would they answer? Consider asking trusted peers and team members the following questions:

    a. How do I present myself (or show up) to others?

    b. Give 3 characteristics (not leadership style) I exhibit in my interactions with others.

    c. What do I do well?

    d. Where can I improve?

    e. What can I do to be more effective as a leader?

3. After stating your leadership style and receiving feedback from trusted allies:

    a. Formulate a plan using SMART (specific, measurable, attainable, relevant, and timed) goals to get from where your allies stated you are as a leader to the leader you wish to become (Ex: If you need to foster better communication with your individual team members, devise a plan to set SMART goal-centric action plan items to meet the goal).

    b. Identify 2-3 trusted allies or mentors who can act as "accountability partners" during your process.

    c. After the initial interaction, follow up in 1, 3, 6, 9, and 12 months (or shorter agreed upon timeframes) with your accountability partners to discuss action plans and your progress in goal attainment.

    d. Revise your action plans as needed to achieve your desired outcome and repeat the process. Document your growth journey and celebrate the small wins you notice!

CHAPTER 7

Understanding Your Emotional Intelligence (or Emotional Quotient)

"Emotional intelligence is a set of skills that help us perceive and understand and effectively respond to emotions." – Dr. Ben Palmer, Genos International

Every human being has emotions. From the day we are born, we exhibit emotions related to how we interpret, relate to, and feel the world around us. From the little baby who cries because she is hungry to the elderly man who is overwhelmed with joy when he is given a surprise 95ᵗʰ birthday party, emotions are a very important and very present part of our being.

Have you heard the saying, "it is not wise to get 'emotional' at work?" If you have, it may have been presented in a manner other than intended. Humans cannot be devoid of emotion regardless of where we are – including the workplace. We cannot remove a portion of our brain and leave it safely tucked away in our cars for 8-12 hours per day until it is acceptable to acknowledge them. Emotions are as much a part of our bodies and existence as our vital organs. The difference is in the control mechanism that supports some functions of our being versus the functioning control of others. For example, organs such as the heart, lungs, and brain function on their own without the constant need for the owner of the parts to remind them to work (involuntary). Those internal organs are autonomic in function. Can you imagine if we had to think to make our hearts beat? What if we had to will each breath before it could be inhaled and exhaled? I may have died a long time ago if I had to remember to take a breath. Thank God these processes are designed to function without our constant input or some of us would be in trouble.

Emotions are different. Emotions can succumb to the will of an individual. Our emotions can be controlled, censored, and honed to appropriately fit circumstances and situations. The key is in knowing how to and when to portray specific emotions and being cognizant of how those displays of emotion will affect those around us.

Understanding Emotional Intelligence

You may have heard or read the words "emotional intelligence" many times in leadership meetings, books, and conferences, but what does that term really mean? Does it mean we hide our emotions and pretend all is well until we reach home where we can unleash on our families? Does it mean we cannot show the emotional aspects of our being while in the workplace or professional environment? Although some may believe this is correct thinking regarding emotional intelligence, this is not humanly possible. Being devoid of emotion implies that a leader or professional would never laugh, never smile, never become upset or disgruntled while in the workplace. As previously stated, this is not humanly possible nor is it a realistic expectation.

Think of a situation where you and another colleague or group did not agree with the proposed plan for an initiative. While your suggestion had evidence-based and research-proven objectives to back its validity, your inappropriate and socially obnoxious coworker repeatedly interrupted your presentation to state his unmerited objections. When you were allowed to state your case and the rationale for your proposed plan and was then was forced to listen to repeated attacks of your ideas and methods by this coworker, how did you feel? Did you have to give yourself an internal pep talk to ensure you did not lash out at the rude individual even in the midst of feeling your neck turn warm? Did you have to work at keeping your tone and your body language appropriate for the venue and audience? After the meeting, did you have to lock yourself in your office to take a few deep breaths or phone a friend to vent while attempting to regain your composure? If so, you have experienced emotions at work. If you have not experienced emotions at work, you more than likely are not human.

Displays of emotion are inevitable. If we stop feeling or experiencing emotions, we are no longer living. The appropriate display of emotions with respect to the witnessing audience and understanding how our responses present to and affect those individuals should be the focus for leaders. This is called emotional intelligence.

Dr. Ben Palmer, President & CEO of Genos International, states,

> "Emotional intelligence is a set of skills that help us perceive and understand and effectively respond to emotions. These skills of emotional intelligence can help us make more informed and better decisions. They can help us interact, communicate, and collaborate more effectively with people, and ultimately, they can help us perform. This is why emotional intelligence is so important in workplaces" (2021).

The Genos International Core Emotional Intelligence (EI) Competencies is a scientific, research-proven concept that defines how individuals react to our environment through demonstrated behaviors that reflect either productive state or nonproductive state behaviors (Genos International, 2021). Scored by a combination of raters, including the individual, peers, direct managers, and direct reports, the Genos EI Leadership Model Competency identifies how the leader presents in six core areas of emotional intelligence: Self-awareness, awareness of others, authenticity, emotional reasoning, self-management, and inspiring performance (Figure 7.1). Each of these EI competencies is evident in all individuals, but some leaders may display productive characteristics while others display nonproductive characteristics related to each competency component. For example, the competency of authenticity has productive and non-productive states. A leader who is seen as authentic is deemed "genuine" on this competency while a leader who is not authentic is seen in the nonproductive state of "untrustworthy." A leader who is scored high in self-management competency is seen as "resilient" while someone who is scored on the lower side of this competency is seen as "temperamental."

Figure 7.1 – Genos International's Models of Emotional Intelligence – The Leadership Model

(Genos International, 2021)

Each of these competencies reflects a leader's ability to either successfully navigate trying situations or unsuccessfully succumb to changes, negative stimuli, and conflicts that may present. Knowing how you are perceived as a leader can assist with reinforcing the positive attributes or refining attitudes, behaviors, and interactions to promote better relationships.

The Influence of the Emotionally Intelligent

> *"Emotional Intelligence can be the game changer to high performance and personal leadership."* – Steve Gutzler

Why is understanding emotional intelligence important? It is important to understand our emotional intelligence (or emotional quotient) and how we are perceived by others because EI affects outcomes, relationships, and potential future prospects. A leader is as good as the team or individuals supporting the leader. A leader who does not have the support, buy-in, and dedication of the team being led will not be as efficient and productive as a leader who is supported and uplifted. Being self-actualized involves being able to see beyond what we want to see or what is favorable in ourselves and either acknowledging and accepting who we are or opting to grow into who we hope to be. Being a person of emotional intelligence follows this same principle. By identifying our current emotional intelligence positioning, devising ways to improve or change it for better, and following through with the identified plan, we can ignite sparks that may change the course of our careers, professions, and lives.

The way we interact with others affects our teams, our peers, those we report to, and how those individuals relate to us. Leaders who are known to be approachable, positive, trustworthy, and supportive have repeatedly presented themselves in a positive manner. Those who are seen as distant, negative, untrustworthy, and unsupportive have shown those characteristics in some form. Peers and team members may not openly recite these phrases when the negative person is in sight, but there is an unspoken culture of fear, intimidation, and distrust within the confines of that individual's professional relationships because of how that person presented in the past.

According to a survey conducted by the Society for Human Resource Management (2020), 1 in 4 Americans dread going to work because of the managers/bosses they work for are not well equipped to handle the stress of their jobs. The lack of training, effectiveness, and ability to effectively lead teams are among some of the most notable deficiencies for management with respect to this study. According to the respondents, the top five skills that managers could improve are communicating effectively (41%), developing and training team members for success (38%), managing time and delegating (37%), cultivating a positive and inclusive team environment (35%), and managing team performance (35%). This equates to more than 1/3 of those surveyed feeling their managers or bosses do not exhibit signs of emotionally intelligent and emotionally aware leaders.

At first glance, the notion that these individuals are not hurting anyone but themselves and halting their own careers may be the sentiment. When a futuristic perspective is taken, the impact of the effectiveness of the team and the prospects of growth and promotion for those being led is also in jeopardy in these situations. For example, if a team is not effective and engaged as a result of the negative impact of those chosen to manage the team, employees may leave. The lack of necessary staffing to efficiently care for the customers may dwindle. The lack of customer service excellence that resulted from the lack of available staff to meet the needs of the customers may be detrimental to the engagement of the team. This lack of team engagement may ultimately result in more individuals leaving the organization and the cycle continues. Not only did the negative behaviors impact the individual displaying the behaviors, but the impact was experienced at levels of the team, the organization, the customers, and the stakeholders. This negative cyclical effect may result from the behaviors and actions of one individual. Think of managers or bosses in your organization that has consistently high turnover rates. This scenario applies.

For leaders who exhibit productive and positive states of emotional intelligence, the opposite effects may be evident. Engaged leaders promote team engagement. Engaged team members usually remain with organizations and give better customer service to clients. Clients who had excellent experiences often retain their relationship with companies that treat them well. These clients may also pass on recommendation to friends, families, and other business associates. The result may be positive for the team, the company, the stakeholders, and the clients. This positive cyclical effect may, in part, be attributed to the presence of an emotionally intelligent and balanced leader.

Most human beings have the capability of being emotionally intelligent. The difference is in the will or the want of the individual. If there is not the will or the want to change to reflect more emotional soundness in professional realms, the outcomes and impact on the peers, teams, and others who interact with that individual will remain the same. The perceptions regarding the individual's leadership or lack thereof will not magically transform until there is a mindset and culture of change in their actions and interactions with others. Making changes in areas that are identified as weaknesses or needing improvement for a manager can assist with changing the overall perception of the team or group.

Leaders' Lesson: How Do I Change How I "Show Up?"

While the process of becoming a person who exhibits emotional intelligence is not an overnight transition, wanting to do better is the first step. Knowing why and how your current state of emotional intelligence affects the feelings, emotions, engagement, and buy-in of a team is the first step in making positive changes. Some of the tips below can assist with reaching greater heights of emotional intelligence.

1. If you have not done so, seek out an executive leadership coach or company that is certified in administering Emotional Intelligence assessments.
2. Ask your peers, team mates, and direct managers to assist in the process of completing the EI assessment. This may be difficult to do, but this input and feedback from those who work closely with you is an integral part of the assessment process.
3. After completion, the certified administrator will review and explain (in detail) the results of the assessment and assist you with identifying action items that will help you improve where needed.
4. Follow the action plan and continue to follow up with your executive coach or certified administrator to ensure accountability and ultimately your developmental and progression goals are met as expected.

CHAPTER 8

Growing YOU: Building
Your Leadership Potential

"To help others develop, start with yourself! When the boss acts like a little god and tells everyone else they need to improve, that behavior can be copied at every level of management. Every level then points out how the level below it needs to change. The end result: No one gets much better." – Marshall Goldsmith

The Importance of Continuous Growth and Self-development

Leadership growth and development is vital to the growth of those around the leader. There are many quotes from exemplary leaders that focus on the importance of taking care of one's own growth to then assist with growing others. The instructions given to passengers on U. S. commercial airline flights can be applied to the importance of self-development of leaders: "Please put on your oxygen mask before attempting to assist others with theirs." To focus solely on developing others without developing self will cause an abrupt halt in the growth of the team.

Think of a phenomenal leader who you met early on during your career and vowed to emulate. Was the person you admired stagnant and static with respect to learning and developing or was that individual constantly trying to improve? Was that individual an avid learner? Was the leader open to and welcoming of feedback from others regarding areas for improvement and further growth? Did watching that leader prompt you to want to do more to develop yourself? A person who has never experienced a leader exhibiting the most appropriate way of handling difficult situations while remaining resilient and optimistic may not know how to invoke or embrace these strong attributes in himself. The process of learning and development will then be viewed as an optional undertaking and the results could be detrimental to the success and sustainability of the team or organization.

Leaders can only develop and support others using a learned, experienced, and developed arsenal of tools that will prepare them for the task at hand. A person who does not know the importance of self-development and its effects on the team will not know how to effectively assist others in developing. We know what we experience. Just as children learn how to interact with the world around them by watching adults' behaviors, attitudes, and relationships, members of a team or workforce learn acceptable and appropriate ways of interacting by watching the behaviors of those they designate as leaders. Leaders are expected to lead by example, not by words alone.

The business world is constantly evolving, growing, changing, and developing. New challenges may present each year. The leaders responsible for ensuring the sustainability of organizations and businesses are responsible for ensuring their personal growth and development modalities meet with the needs and demands of those challenges.

Developing Self

> *"Leadership and learning are indispensable to each other"* –
> John F. Kennedy

There are various methods of leadership development that can be used for self-development and growth. These include (but are not limited to) organizational offerings, individual studies, and on-the-job learning processes.

Organization-sponsored Leadership Development Programs

In recent decades, the importance of leadership development has become evident for many executives. It is now known that leaders who continue to develop themselves and grow their leadership prowess are more effective and thus create more desirable outcomes for organizations. As a result, many business organizations offer some form of leadership development to management level employees. These programs may be optional or mandatory, self-paced or structured in nature, but all are designed to promote success of the leaders within the organization. For sectors of business where it is imperative for leaders to continue to grow with the challenges and changes that frequently present, the need for leadership development programs is most important.

According to Sonnino (2016),

> "The concept of leadership has evolved from the top-down, paternalistic model, where the leader is in complete control and demands performance from others, to a more collaborative approach, where the leader helps his/her team develop a vision and empowers them to accomplish the stated goals. Many have suggested that formal training in the multifaceted components of leadership is necessary and should begin at an early career stage, yet still today, the number of

comprehensive leadership training opportunities, at any career level, is limited" (Journal of Healthcare Leadership, para 2.).

Alternatives to Organizational Leadership Development Programs

Although it is apparent that leadership development programs are necessary to promote better outcomes for leaders, teams, and organizations, many organizations still struggle with incorporating effective and timely leadership development programs into their portfolio of institutional learning. Why is it difficult for some to maintain leadership development programs for their management teams? There are two most probable deterrents: Time and Cost.

For some organizations, acquiring organizational leadership development teams is feasible. For larger scale organizations, the ability to payroll and utilize these content experts is a no-brainer and requires little hardship. The programs are usually incorporated into the routine workday and are usually marketed only to management-level team members. This eliminates the need for making time concessions and finding replacement workers for frontline employees who are vital to the day-to-day operations of the business. Unfortunately, this drastically decreases the potential for those on the frontline who have the bones to be strong leaders from participating in the learning and development courses.

For other organizations, the inability to obtain dedicated, certified, and capable organization-based leadership development experts may force many business executives to consider other options. Those who seek out leadership development courses for their management teams may be forced to look to alternative (and more costly) learning modalities. Organizations may opt to contract with leadership development experts for larger, corporate seminar-type learning modalities that are streamlined to their teams' needs. These programs may work well for large corporations and those with a liberal cash flow, but smaller companies may not be able to afford expensive learning processes and may vote to eliminate developmental training programs altogether.

Many organizations prefer to sponsor employees who wish to attend leadership development conferences to assist with promoting the development process. For some executives, the option of reimbursement is a good way to support employees who wish to attend leadership development-centric programs, but the up-front expenses and costs associated with attending the events may cause those who wish to attend to decide otherwise. Other companies expect their leaders to take on the responsibility of paying for these "optional" programs themselves. In these cases, leadership development may be seen as the sole responsibility of those individuals who agree to pay out-of-pocket for such training.

Self-sponsored Leadership Development

There are various methods of leadership development that can be used to reach the leader's goals. These processes may include formal and informal methods of learning. Some examples of commonly sought out learning opportunities include self-paced virtual or distance learning programs and in-person seminars and conferences. While these modalities are important for the development of leaders, there are alternate, ways to assist with self-development and leadership growth. These include networking, professional organization membership, volunteer opportunities, and committee/initiative planning opportunities.

Networking – One of the most efficient (and often underappreciated) ways to meet leaders who may have a vital impact in the development of other leaders is by networking. The process of networking may be seen by some as a way to get contacts who will assist with moving from A to B position or as a way to get to know those who may introduce us to other "movers and shakers" within organizations. For some leaders, this process can become daunting because of the inevitable, "who can you introduce me to who can push my career forward" mentality that sometimes presents during the networking process. While making professional connections is important, networking, if done correctly, can yield much more than a "thanks for the business card" opportunity. Yes, networking can be used to form an alliance with those who may assist us with being seen by the "right people," but the ultimate goal of networking is to create a synergistic relationship between multiple individuals or entities for the purpose of strengthening and supporting one another. The relationship should be symbiotic and should flow in both directions. It should be beneficial to both parties. The lack of this mentality has caused many to deem networking a necessary evil when it can be a blessing.

The networking opportunity can be used not only to ask for introductions to other leaders, but as an opportunity to learn from those in the network without asking for "favors." Many of my colleagues have shunned the local networking events because of the unending "what can you do for me" interactions that abound. For many leaders, the opportunity to get to know more about an individual's drive and passion is more engaging than being asked to pass a business card to the next highest officer. Showing the want and will to grow and develop is more appealing and welcoming to executives and leaders who are looking for great connections that may eventually lead to more. If a potential networking opportunity presents itself, asking if there is an opportunity for project collaboration or if the leader would be available to discuss strategies related to business processes that affect the community you both serve may be a better lead-in. This method of introduction shows professionalism as well as passion for growth, collaboration, and development. Asking to help instead of asking for help is the best way to prevent your business card from being thrown into the discard pile after the networking event ends. Invest in long-term relationships.

Professional Organization Membership – Being a member of a professional organization is not solely a method of sprucing up a resume. Professional organization membership can be a very effective way of growing in the profession. The information, bonds, and relationships formed within the confines of professional organizations may assist leaders in building a strong support system of like-minded colleagues within the same field of business. This can lead to opportunities to communicate and collaborate with those who are experts in the business field. Using professional organizations as a means of growth and development is key to continuing to evolve as a leader. The key is to get involved. There are many learning opportunities within professional organizations. Don't just join a professional organization – get involved!

The intricate inclusion of individuals within professional organizations is vast. These networks usually include executives from various organizations who are willing to give information, insight, and industry tips to the professional members and vice versa. What we may not be privy to or what may not be safe to openly discuss at work (because of rank or title restrictions) may ultimately be presented and discussed to some degree with within the professional organization venue. For example, issues that arise at work on the executive level may not be divulged to those on lower levels of the organizational chart. Certain aspects of executive management are discussed within conference rooms and that information may be dispersed to limited personnel within the organization. The intricacies of operations may never be discussed with some who would like to learn from hearing those details. The beauty of the professional organization is that there is no level of importance among members. Regardless of their station within organizations, executives, chiefs, frontline team members, managers, etc., are purposely intermingled. This allows conversations and collaboration that transcends rank or title. The result is shared learnings for all involved. The learning events create a vast array of both networking and development opportunities. Most professional organizations hold annual conferences where the reach of the local chapter of the organization can be exponentially extended. For leaders who are motivated to seek out self-development processes, there is a wide array of programs and learning events that are offered by professional organizations.

Volunteer Opportunities – Throughout this section of learning, the theme has been the same: Get involved. The more visible a leader is, the more opportunity for growth, development, and even discovery there will be. During a past coaching session that focused on leadership development opportunities, a client discussed the prospect of volunteer opportunities and wondered if volunteering would promote learning and development. My response was, "absolutely."

While some may see volunteering as something to occupy time or to give back, volunteering can also yield a return for the volunteer. Volunteering is multi-faceted. You may volunteer within your organization or in a community-based setting.

Volunteering for opportunities is a way to grow your skills as a leader. Pushing beyond what is comfortable to take on a role that invokes contemplation, thinking, and even a bit of a struggle can assist leaders with becoming stronger and more resilient in other matters. Volunteering to assist on projects on subjects which you may not be well-informed will promote learning. Researching and seeking out those with more expertise can assist with becoming familiar with the content while growing your knowledge, resiliency, and fortitude as a leader. As an athlete must push beyond her current level of comfort to stretch her muscles to higher levels of growth and strength, a leader must stretch beyond his comfort zone in order to grow and develop his leadership strengths. Be comfortable getting uncomfortable.

Volunteering by giving back to the community can assist with leadership skills and development as well as allow the participant to touch others they may not meet otherwise. For example, as a healthcare leader, volunteering at health fairs where I interact with other leaders while caring for the community we serve is a spiritual experience. While we fight for the rights and better access to care for those in our communities takes place in a corporate environment, being able to relate to and interact with those in our communities gives us real, personal understanding of the struggles that our clients encounter. This results in more passion, more drive, more determination, and more responsibility to meet the needs of those needing help.

This experience is not central to healthcare nor is it confined to one industry. In most urban metropolises, those who work in Information Technology fields have the opportunity to volunteer at community centers where those with limited computer knowledge and skills may gather to learn how to apply for jobs online. Those who are in academia may volunteer their expertise to help illiterate adults learn to read and write. Many who own restaurants volunteer in parks on weekends to feed homeless populations in inner city limits. Some who are skilled at barbering or cosmetology often volunteer in underserved populations to give free haircuts and makeovers to low-income neighborhood children at the start of the school year. These skilled leaders also volunteer throughout the year to prepare homeless individuals for job interviews. Those who volunteer are exposed to many in the community who are likeminded and dedicated to empowering others. Those who are known for their leadership at these events are asked to participate in other community-based events and initiatives, which extends the opportunity for growth and development. The opportunities to help others while learning to grow your leadership skills are endless.

Committee Involvement – Within organizations, leaders may seek out opportunities to get close to those they wish to learn from. Committee participation is one of the best ways to experience an array of leaders at work. Volunteering for committees exposes leaders to others within the organization that they may not encounter otherwise. Leaders who are seeking out opportunities for growth without a monetary expense may benefit from committee involvement.

"Leader watching" is a viable way to learn how to conquer problems and issues while developing leadership prowess and skill. Looking to those whom we deem "experts" or "leaders" is a common aspect of learning and development. Many who sit on committees have either volunteered for the opportunity or have been assigned to committees because of their ability to motivate others to get results. These strong leaders are often open to sharing their knowledge by mentoring others to lead as they do. While the main objective of the committee is to reach the goals set by the entity, the possibility of learning how to interact with and motivate others to do their best may be realized during committee participation.

The key to committee involvement is to find committees that interest you. If you need to grow in an area of expertise, do not limit yourself to what is familiar. Be comfortable stretching yourself into realms that may seem daunting at first. What eludes us can help us grow if we put in the work. If used correctly, committee involvement can be the way to further self-development and increased opportunities in the future.

Leaders' Lesson: How Can You Develop Self?

As we end this chapter, it is important to reiterate the need for leaders to continually grow and develop. Each day should bring about a situation or lesson that we can use to grow our leadership strengths and capabilities. When we cease growing, we are no longer effective. It is imperative for leaders to seek out opportunities for further growth and development. Whether these are instituted by an organization or self-instituted and sought out for individual-driven development, leaders must be vigilant in looking for ways to improve beyond the current state.

Contemplate the following before moving to the next chapter:

1. How can you grow and develop yourself to ensure you are prepared to assist in developing others?
2. Identify three areas of your leadership portfolio that need additional focus.
3. Using the three identified areas above, what steps can you take starting today that will stretch your leadership strengths beyond comfortable limits?

CHAPTER 9

Showing Up Successful –
You're Always On Stage!

"The key to successful leadership today is influence, not authority." – Ken Blanchard

Knowing How to Use Your Leadership Influence

We can learn a lot by simply watching those around us. How a leader acts, reacts, and interacts tells those watching of the true strength and veracity of the leader. What leaders expect from those who follow and rely on them must be first be exhibited by those leaders. Our influence is only as good as our actions. Our words become pointless if they do not align with the actions we exhibit. Regardless of what we say, what we model is what we believe. People pay closer attention to our actions that they ever will to our words. Our true influence is in our actions. We must act accordingly.

Knowing how to use leadership influence is imperative for success. Unfortunately, HR-given authority is often mistaken for leadership influence. Authority causes the unwilling yielding to the will of another to comply with mandated power. Influence is an effect on the characteristics, development and behaviors, attitudes, or beliefs of another. Bosses rely on authority to demand compliance while leaders rely on influence.

The need for some management-level employees to be highly "boss-centric" (or authoritarian) and constantly "in control" causes many to fear instead of respect and support those to whom they report. The need for some management-level employees to continue the authoritarian style of management has caused many to leave organizations for better working relationships and less stressful situations. A Gallup (2015) study of 2.5 million manager-led teams surveyed over four decades revealed that 1 in 2 people admitted to leaving companies to get away from managers. This longitudinal study also showed that many of those who remain in unfavorable manager-employee relationships are disengaged and do not perform to their full potential.

The use of leadership influence versus appointed authority has the potential of changing the outlook and culture of a team. Leaders who use influence to promote the greater good of the team can ignite sparks throughout the team that may spread throughout the organization. Leaders who are focused on influencing those they are blessed to lead instead of dictating and invoking consistent authoritarian forms of power may promote the willing agreement and support of their teams. The key is in knowing how and when to use influence over authority. There is a delicate balance.

As mentioned in previous chapters, there are times when leaders must be more authoritative in nature. In situations where time is of the essence and upper management-mandated quick changes and implementations are necessary, there is little room for discussion or debate. For those who are highly influential and approachable in day-to-day situations, the infrequent use of authoritative power may not invoke feelings of fear and intimidation from team members. The relationship between the team and the leader or boss dictates the outcome. For example, a leader who is known as influential because of her ability to consistently inspire, uplift, empower, and support her team may need to present in an authoritative manner to get a specific task completed within a short timeframe. Because of the history of the respectful and supportive relationship built between the leader and the team, this incident more than likely will not have a negative impact on the relationship of the group. The team is more inclined to understand when situations require more definite and directive modes of action and because of their respect for the leader, compliance and buy-in may be easily obtained.

In contrast, for managers who are highly authoritarian and consistently use authority and power to yield results and compliance, the response is often negative. The boss who is consistently authoritarian and uses authority or HR-appointed "power" to relate to employees will also yield compliance from the team, but for different reasons. The boss's employees are often exposed to this controlling and "my way or no way" mode of management from the boss; therefore, the yield will be different. The task will be performed out of fear and the engagement and buy-in will more than likely not exist. The outcomes may look similar, yet the bilateral relationship of two-way respect and support is not present. Why does this relationship matter? This matters because employee engagement matters.

Influence and Employee Engagement

Employee engagement (the desire for employees to be physically, emotionally, and relationally present to ensure what is needed to move the team and organization forward is performed) is more prevalent in teams where leaders are supportive, influential, appreciative, and respectful of teams' work. As leaders have known for decades, those who are better engaged yield better outcomes for organizations. The use of authoritarian and "I'm the boss" primary management styles negatively influences employee engagement. Although this type of management style may have been acceptable in earlier decades, it is not acceptable, nor favorable for many organizations in the 21st century. Managers account for nearly 70% of the variance related to employee engagement. The impact of lower engagement at the hands of U. S. managers translated to losses of between $319-398 billion (Gallup, 2015). A recent Gallup engagement report shows worldwide engagement results of 21% for employees, which means that only 1 in 5 employees in the world are reportedly engaged employees (Gallup, 2022). Much of this is also at the hand of managers. Simply put, adults have options and people who report to "bad managers" often leave for better working conditions in other companies. Those who are allowed to display ongoing authoritarian behaviors may cause organizations to experience less favorable employee engagement scores and are more inclined to have higher levels of employee turnover and customer dissatisfaction. Both of these elements affect the bottom line or profit margin of organizations.

Leadership influence is a gift, not a right. Leaders understand that influence should not be assumed or expected because of a position or rank but it is given by those who follow the leader out of respect, loyalty, and support for what the leader does and how the leader presents. Leaders should use the gift of influence to positively affect the outcomes of the whole, not to gain notoriety, fame, or self-centered accolades. The influence of a leader should be seen as a sacred offering between members of a team and the leader. It should be used and respected as such. Leaders should uplift, uphold, support, and promote their teams by using the influence gifted to move team-centric objectives and goals in a positive, team-beneficial direction. Using influence in any other method or for any other outcome is not leadership.

Remaining Resilient and Optimistic During Tough Times

"Do not judge me by my success, judge me by how many times I fell down and got back up again." – Nelson Mandela

It is often said that we can tell the strength of a person's character by watching how that person reacts during times of turmoil. People are often judged by their response to untoward situations and circumstances. This is true in most aspects of life. Have you ever attended a funeral or memorial service and watched intently to see how the grieving family would react? Maybe you watched the First Family as they buried their beloved husband, father, brother, and friend, President John F. Kennedy. Do you remember hearing the commentators of various media outlets state how "strong" the First Family was as they endured the heart-wrenching processions that occurred on that day? Think back to a situation where you witnessed someone in a position of leadership respond to unsatisfactory news. How did that person react? What about a boxer who repeatedly gets knocked to the mat by his opponent only to stand up again and face another blow? Did you think, "wow, he's resilient" as the person continued to pick himself up during the match or did you think, "what a weakling" as the person fought time and time again against the obstacle in his way?

As stated by Nelson Mandela, our strength is often found in how we "get back up" after a devastating blow. Resiliency is the ability to continue to fight, push, and struggle through difficulty. The goal of a leader is not to avoid difficult situations. This is not possible in any realm of life. We will have difficulty. We will struggle. We may even fall during the battle, but the key is to resolve to get back up again. Our strength is not defined by how we fall, but by how we get back up.

The Bible is saturated with similar messages of resiliency to the ages. Why is that? Because it is inevitable that human beings will fall at some point during their lives. This fall may be related to a substance abuse issue, infidelity, loss of a loved one, divorce, loss of a home or property, navigating a chronic illness, being passed over for a promotion or job, or an entrepreneurial business failure. Regardless of which situation applies to your life, every human being has or will experience a fall or discouraging moment of some sort. There are some who may resolve to give in and succumb to the fall while others will fight against the obstacle and push on against all odds. The choice is an individual one. The fall does not have to be the period at the end of any story. Some will see the fall as the event before the comma. The story will go on for many. This is a determining and defining factor in whether someone is a strong and resilient leader or a person who lives to be conquered by circumstances. As relayed by the Biblical Hebrew prophet Micah, we may fall down, but we will get back up (Micah 7:8).

Resilience is a crucial characteristic of high-performing leaders. Resilient leaders have the ability to sustain their energy level under pressure to cope with disruptive changes and adapt (Kohlrieser, 2014). Being resilient does not mean we do not feel pain, sorrow, or hurt related to devastation and loss. Leaders are not inhuman. Leaders feel the same pain and hurt that others experience when situations do not pan out as planned. Although leaders may press on and get up from devastating situations and circumstances that push them down, they may still have bruises and scars to mark those dark occasions that caused them to fall. For example, someone who has endured the heartache that accompanies a failed business strategy will always remember the feelings of hurt, disappointment, embarrassment, and discouragement surrounding that traumatic event. Leaders are not immune to these emotions or feelings. The difference is in how a leader reacts after the event has ended. Do leaders wallow in the hurt or resolve to learn from it?

How the leader reacts in times of failure is directly related to how those being led will respond. In situations where conflict is persistent and outcomes are not as expected, leaders are watched intently to see how they will respond. People who look to leaders for guidance and answers to "what now" or "what happens next" will follow what is being shown. The leader's ability to remain resilient is critical at these crossroads because the response will either help or discourage those watching. Team members who witness these events and the reaction of leaders are either discouraged by the behaviors of the leader or encouraged and inspired to emulate the ability of the leader to learn from mistakes and failures and build on those learning experiences. In other words, the adage "follow the leader" applies in this scenario.

If we wish to teach our teams and those looking to us as leaders to be resilient during difficulties, we must prove ourselves to be resilient. This is done by modeling characteristics of a resilient leader. The lack of resiliency will result in not only failure of the one designated to lead, but failure of the team as well. If we cannot model resiliency for those who depend on us, we cannot expect our teams and followers to be resilient during the difficult times. Model resiliency and the yield will be resiliency.

Social Media Presence – You Can't Take That Back!

Social media is a very prevalent means of communication in the 21st century. Most people participate in or are members of at least one form of social media communication outlet. Whether it is YouTube community, Facebook, or LinkedIn, most people have some sort of link to what is going on in the world around them. These media outlets can be very beneficial for keeping abreast of world happenings, family events, and business communications, but the outlets are also used as forms of inappropriate and unnerving and misleading communication from those who are given free access to post, blog, vlog, or comment on social media sites. As leaders, we must be cognizant of what we are being linked to in social media realms.

The Reach of Social Media and Its Impact on Leaders

For leaders, social media is a tricky tool. While social media sites are often used to promote businesses and positive communications regarding family trips and friends' achievements, social media also hosts those who wish to promote the dark side of society. The effects of the latter can reach far beyond the post of the person who wishes to expose darkness to the world. The reach can be extended to all in that person or entity's social media community.

A close friend recalled an incident that played out on social media. A former friend who she was at odds with consistently posted information regarding a personal situation that painted my friend in a negative light within her family. This resulted in an argument and unsavory words being passed from person to person. Unfortunately, not only did the family members witness these interactions, but those in both individuals' professional realms were privy to the content being splayed across the social media pages as well. This resulted in people within my close friend's workplace having very personal information about their peer and coworker, which resulted in negative professional outcomes for her. Even though the nature of the argument that was displayed on social media was personal, it became impossible to separate the personal from the professional once the information was handed to everyone listed as contacts on the social media site. Although the ladies eventually removed the content from the website, the damage was already done.

Have you experienced waking up and reading negative comments about yourself or someone you knew being posted for all on social media to view? Have you had to block someone from your social media sites because of comments made regarding another race, religion, political party, or group of people? Have you had to remove someone from the ability of seeing or posting information on your page because of their venomous comments? I have experienced friends and business colleagues who were shunned because someone in their social media communities posted racially-charged and anti-LGBTQ+-focused hate posts on their sites. Those who were associated with these leaders saw the posts as offensive and inappropriate. The owners of the feed were targeted as being the ones promoting hate because of what they allowed in their feeds. This is a common occurrence on social media. Even if you may not be the poster, what is displayed on your page represents you for those who visit your site. Be cautious in what you allow and who you allow to enter your life via social media outlets.

Those we allow access to our social media lives suddenly have access into our business and personal lives as well. It is imperative to take caution before allowing the world to access our lives. Many see social media as a separate presence that should not affect or change business interactions and relationships, but human beings have very little ability to separate business and personal identities when negative information arises. Some thrive on taking the negative and bringing others down with it. Take for example the politicians who post racially-charged and hate-slathered posts on social media only to remove the posts the next day after receiving numerous comments from angry constituents. Even though an apology may be issued, the verbiage is already out in the world. It has been seen, commented on, and passed to thousands for viewing. The actions of that person have already been displayed and negative traits that may have otherwise been hidden have been uncovered for the world to see. Apologies aside, the negativity cannot be taken back. Many have lost their livelihoods and families secondary to one social media rant or post that was not well considered prior to hitting "send."

Once information is posted online in social media forms, it is viewed by hundreds and passed on to others within in a matter of minutes (depending on the source of the information). This is a far reach into the community and ultimately the world. Regardless of whether or not the post is removed from the online forum, if it has been viewed and shared by those in our professional and personal realms, the damage and after-effects can be long term.

Prevention of Untoward Posts

Leaders must ensure that they remain cognizant of the impact of social media and how it can affect personal and business interactions. If social media is used, leaders must ensure they are paying close attention to what someone else may be posting in their threads and eliminating those sources of negativity, hatred, and ill-will that are posted online. This should be a common practice to prevent negative and inappropriate posts to be fed into leaders' social media sites. Here are a few steps to ensure you are not allowing harmful thoughts and actions to be captured in your feed:

1. Do not allow people into your social media circles if you are not familiar with their character or content of their online image. Peruse the pages of those who are asking for access to your feeds before accepting invitations. This quick research process can prevent later damage.
2. Be cognizant of what is posted on or pulled into your feed via social media sites. Check your sites often to ensure the content you have allowed in your feed is appropriate.
3. Once you witness something that is not in line with your beliefs, remove it or take it down before it can cause further damage.
4. If you feel there is need for more conversation regarding a negative or improper post about you or your loved ones,

DO NOT RESPOND ONLINE. Take the conversation offline. Use other means of communicating with the other party instead of displaying arguments and inappropriate language via social media. Omit the audience and discuss the matter in private or simply remove the source of the negativity from being able to contact you or post in your feed.

5. Quickly communicate any issues or untoward activity with those in your circle. Be candid regarding the origination of the negative feeds or posts and assure your contacts that you have removed the source of the negativity from allowed posts.

6. If needed, contact the administrator of the site to ask for quick assistance in removing the post or blocking the individual from further accessing your page.

Although policing our social media sites can be a daunting task, it is necessary to prevent backlash and reprimand by those in personal, social, and professional aspects of our lives. Social media is a large aspect of our lives in the 21st century; therefore, we as leaders must treat it with the same tenacity and influence as our words. We must remain vigilant regarding appropriateness of what we post or allow on social media outlets. The results of not doing so could be irreparable damage to our character and reputations.

Leaders' Lesson: Practical Application

Throughout this chapter, we discussed ways in which leaders can be more influential, remain resilient, and limit the negative impact of social media. Think on these questions as you prepare to move to the next chapter.

1. How can I show my influence in a manner that is respectful and supportive?
2. What steps can I take that will have a larger impact on those I lead?
3. Think back to a time when you failed to reach a goal or you were confronted with devastating outcomes on a project or initiative. How did you respond to that incident? What did you learn?
4. What can you do to ensure you show resilience as a leader?
5. What aspects of social media presence do you need to revise? What areas should you omit to ensure negativity and unexpected outcomes do not present?

PART IV

Developing More Leaders
- Growing Others

"I start with the premise that the function of leadership is to produce more leaders, not more followers." – Ralph Nader

The goal of any leader should be to develop more leaders. The focus of a leader is to bring about positive change and outcomes. Leaders must ensure that those who are deemed followers or team members today can take on the task of leading others tomorrow. We learned that leaders must continue to develop, learn, and grow themselves in preparation for growing those who follow them. This is a concurrent process and occurs in the same realm of time. Leaders are consistently growing and developing. While this important work is being performed and experienced, leaders are expected to grow those who depend on them for guidance and support. The result is growth for all, not just one.

How do leaders develop more leaders? How do leaders prepare those destined to lead for the important task of doing so? By offering assistance, listening, and living the example of a leader.

Offer Yourself Up: How Can I Help?

Leaders often know which team members are destined to be great leaders themselves. The act of watching a group can uncover the traits, characteristics, and behaviors in some that make them more prone to become leaders. Leaders must work diligently to prepare the next generation of leaders for greatness. One important role of a leader is to use the knowledge, experiences, and pearls of wisdom that they possess to develop others.

There are many processes to preparing a person to take on the challenges of a new undertaking. Precepting and training is one phase of the process. Precepting and training processes are instituted at the beginning of a new work relationship. Precepting and training involve teaching someone the aspects of a job or duty to assist with the tasks assigned to that individual being carried out as expected. These processes are usually related to a job onboarding process. These mechanisms of learning are instituted by human resources and educational departments within organizations. The precepting and training processes include an employee being assigned to another more skilled and experienced employee who can act as a guide to walk the new employee through steps of processes, policies, etc. This process is not a voluntary undertaking and is considered a part of the more experienced employee's job duties. This is an integral and very important aspect of preparing an individual for a new role.

Unlike precepting or training, mentoring relationships take on a different concept. While precepting and training are elements of onboarding or mandatory educational pursuits within organizations, mentoring is usually a voluntary process that is not instituted by human resource mechanisms. Most commonly, mentoring can be instituted by individuals who seek out assistance or guidance from others within the organization who have proven themselves as leaders. In some cases, human resources may encourage mentoring relationships to form, but the standard mentoring relationship is sought out by those seeking mentoring.

Mentoring is often confused with precepting and training, but it is vastly different. Mentoring is a process of sharing, developing, supporting, and advising that is used to grow a person in a specific area or set of skills. Mentoring is a means of development that transcends the defined aspects of precepting and training. Precepting or training is defined by limitations in time (e.g., 2 weeks at the beginning of a new job or learning process). Mentoring may be a lifelong commitment. Precepting may involve someone teaching another a specific job skill. Mentoring involves the development of various abilities, regardless of job involvement. Precepting is highly technique-focused. Mentoring is mindset-focused. Preceptors must report findings to those who manage the new employee. Mentors have a trusting, transparent relationship with mentees and the responsibility of accountability lies within that relationship.

Leaders are usually sought out to be mentors for others who seek guidance and unbiased, candid input for their development, learning, and growth. Those seeking mentoring relationships may have watched the leader's behaviors, interactions, and reactions before approaching the leader for consideration. Because this process is not usually an HR-driven process, the approach of a potential mentee to a potential leader may cause anxiety. It is not easy to ask someone to take you under their wing and assist you with becoming a stronger, more effective person. The possibility that the leader may decline the opportunity or may see the person seeking the mentoring relationship in a negative manner may be a deterrent to those who wish to seek out such engagements. It can be a scary and very transparent experience for someone seeking mentoring.

For a leader, the prospect of acquiring someone who wishes to use the relationship as a means of promotion to higher positions at the hand of the mentor may be a reason for not wishing to move forward with the mentoring process. If the leader has experienced negative mentoring interactions in the past, the prospect of taking on a new mentee may not be favorable. Leaders may have experienced mentees who were not dedicated to the process and may have weighed heavily on the time, energy, and knowledge of the mentor. Some may have abused or disrespected the time of the mentor. Instead of mentees being prepared and respecting the time of the mentor, some may treat the relationship haphazardly and cause the mentor to retire from mentoring engagements. These types of interactions can ruin potential future mentoring relationship prospects for others. If a leader has experienced a negative or less than favorable mentoring relationship, the leader must try to limit the negative connotations of that experience to that experience alone. While it may be difficult to do, it is imperative for leaders to offer themselves to others to ensure great leadership energy and expertise is passed from one generation of leaders to another.

Many of us may have experienced the negative mentoring relationship either as mentors or mentees. Some may have vowed not to mentor or engage with mentees after those events. Please do not block others from experiencing your positivity and guidance based on past experiences. The negative mentoring experience can serve as a learning opportunity. The lessons that leaders can extract from those negative mentoring instances involve knowing what behaviors to avoid as mentors and mentees. If a mentor was negative, did not show up for agreed upon meet ups, or did not turn out to be a good role model, that outcome can be used to guide others in the correct way of showing up as a leader. If a mentee was disrespectful of time and efforts of you as the mentor, teaching your mentee how to respect and appreciate the time and efforts of others who are willing to assist with their growth and development can benefit the mentee. As leaders, growth comes not only from positive outcomes but also from negative ones. There is a lesson in everything we experience. Even though some experiences in mentoring may have been negative, others may prove to be great mentees and may go on to mentor others by using the lessons learned while under the leader's guidance. Leaders take the good and the bad and use both to grow. Offer up your abilities and expertise as a mentor and assist others with growing and developing into leaders who will be appropriate to sit where you currently sit.

Listen More than You Speak

Communication is a two-way mechanism of exchanging information. One party must listen and the other party must relay what is intended to be shared in order for communication to be effective. This is evident not only in human relationships, but in nature all around us. I enjoy taking fast-paced walks around my neighborhood because it allows me to witness the most underappreciated element of life: Nature. Watching how animals, birds, and insects interact with one another and how they communicate and follow through with tasks is amazing. Have you witnessed a group of birds communicating while maintaining distance between them? Birds will sit in various trees along a street or in a forested area and take turns communicating to ensure all in their party are aware of the plan for their course or the lay of the land they wish to traverse. One bird gawks their communication while others listen intently. Once that bird finishes communicating, there's silence for a few moments. The others remain quiet in what seems like an effort to give another time to speak. Watching this phenomenon week after week caused me to ponder why human beings do not follow the notions of nature.

You may have heard the saying (maybe from your mom), "God gave you one mouth and two ears for a reason! Listen twice as much as you speak!" This is true in leadership as well. Just as nature teaches us many lessons, if we listen from time to time, we can gain better insights into the world around us. Being a great leader includes knowing when to speak and when to listen. Some may believe that leaders must have the answer to every problem and should interject themselves in every situation to prove their expertise. This is not the case. Great leaders know when to speak and when to listen.

I had the honor of watching one of the greatest leaders I have ever worked with practice this process in action. I attended a meeting of critical care managers, directors, and medical directors in a hospital where I worked. Some of the behaviors exhibited and attitudes presented during that meeting were less than acceptable. My first thought was that I needed to prove my strength by showing that I could match and then surpass what was being acted out by those in the meeting. I was prepared to defend the input of those who were obviously right in that matter. For some reason, I did not respond. I looked to my critical care director and noticed her demeanor. I watched as my critical care director, Kelly Heathman, appropriately expressed herself while maintaining her composure and without displaying negative emotion during the berating and unprofessional verbiage that was spewed out regarding our staff. While I could tell she was not in agreement with what was being exhibited in the meeting, she did not match the negativity or emotional charge of those who deemed themselves leaders. She stated what needed to be said and maintained her silence until after the meeting was adjourned. Initially, I thought we had failed in proving ourselves in that meeting.

I followed my director back to her office and listened intently as she made a phone call to one of the self-proclaimed "leaders" who was adamant about belittling and berating the nursing staff during the meeting. I watched as she released what I thought she was more than justified in releasing during the meeting. I suddenly realized that her strength was not in her comeback or the trading of inappropriate words while seated in a room of executive and providers. Her strength was not in "saving face" and witty, snide remarks. Her strength was in her silence. While others ranted and raved about an issue we knew we were right on, she stated her input and took a very difficult position: One of a respectful listener in the midst of the rambling. My respect for her did not wane because of her silence. It heightened. I learned a valuable lesson during that meeting because of the strength of my leader and her ability to listen to inappropriate comments being relayed even when she knew she was right.

If they are being honest, many leaders may admit that they wish they would have held back from speaking too quickly or responding to swiftly to something that was said or done in the past. Many have responded in rage to issues, events, or circumstances that may have been resolved using other means if they would have listened and held back their emotions long enough to think about the outcomes prior to acting. Does this make those leaders less efficient or less than leaders? No. This makes them human. Listening is not easy for those who are accustomed to giving advice and input as leaders are, but leaders learn to effectively communicate when situations are tense. Listening to others' input during situations when we feel we have the answers is difficult to do. It takes restraint to listen without interruption. This does not mean that leaders will not make mistakes, will not respond too quickly to an off-putting email, and will not rush to judgement before getting the full story when emotions run high. Everyone makes mistakes. Whether we grow from them or continue on the same negative path dictates if we are leaders or not.

Effective listening is a skill that leaders must possess. As an executive coach, this did not come as an easy skill for me. Having been a nurse for well over two decades, I was accustomed to giving the answers and solving the problems instead of listening to the input and ideas of others. During training processes for my coaching certifications, I learned the importance of listening and waiting for others to give input into what they identified as viable solutions to issues and problems. I learned that others can provide insight into issues and problems even if the means of solving the problem did not coincide with my revelations. To come to this conclusion, I had to learn the art of effective listening.

Effective listening is an art that involves being able to put aside our thoughts, ideas, viewpoints, and input to welcome the thoughts, ideas, viewpoints, and input from another. Listening is an important skill for leaders to develop. Leaders who listen intently and actively without constantly thinking of an appropriate response, rebuttal, or comeback exhibit more character and strength than people who push their words and opinions on others without consideration of others' input. As leaders, we must learn to listen more than we speak. If people feel like they are being heard, they are more inclined to talk. Those who feel like they have a voice are more engaged in the work and tasks that must be performed. Leaders who exhibit a preference for listening are rated as significantly more effective than those who spend the majority of their time talking *at* their employees.

Effective listening requires self-training. When we practice active listening, we are asking our brains to absorb what is being said by the speaker. It is not something that comes naturally to everyone (Warstrom, 2020). Leaders must practice and hone this skill to ensure it is well developed and cultivated. Leaders who train themselves to take a back seat and listen as opposed to being behind the wheel and controlling the destination allow for the growth and development of others. Leaders who exhibit this relinquishing of control in conversations, meetings, and interactions with team members are more prone to earn the respect of their followers. This practice also presents the prospect of team members being willing to share their thoughts, ideas, and input into what works and what changes may benefit the team and the organization.

Lead by Example – Do What I Do

The most important element of leadership is found in our actions. There are many great leaders who may speak eloquently or stir passion and emotions within a crowd by giving speeches that can ignite a spark within the hearts of those who hear it. There are many who are excellent orators and can bring groups of individuals to tears by relaying their feelings, passions, and mantras to others. While these elements of leadership may be useful in pushing positive responses and actions that incite change in others, what leaders do is the most powerful tool to promote reinforcement of positive behaviors.

Having worked in healthcare for many years, I have watched physicians, nurses, and respiratory therapists, and others attempt to coerce patients who had lung cancer, Chronic Obstructive Pulmonary Disease (COPD), and other respiratory diseases to stop smoking. Those conversations were very moving and the patients and some of their family members stated they understood the critical need to stop smoking if they wished to recover from the horrible illnesses they were battling. During one such conversation, one of my patients became upset for no apparent reason. The patient listened while the respiratory therapist continued to tell him of the benefits of smoking cessation and how that process could help him recover. I was in the room preparing the patient's medications during that conversation. As the therapist continued to relay facts that he was trained to hand to the patient, the patient suddenly stopped the therapist mid-sentence. I listened as the patient asked the therapist, "Man, how are you going to tell me I shouldn't smoke, but I see you standing outside smoking every time I'm out there smoking. You smell like smoke right now!" The therapist went on to say that he was not sick and the education was for the patient. The patient dismissed the therapist from the room and asked me to prevent him from returning. I did as I was asked.

When the therapist approached me later that shift and attempted to downplay what the patient stated, I responded by saying, "You cannot convince a person to stop doing what is harmful if you are doing that same behavior." The respiratory therapist was not happy to hear my input, but he knew the patient was correct in his rebuttal.

You may have experienced this same phenomenon when interacting with your children. Maybe you overheard one of your children use an inappropriate word when speaking with a playmate of a sibling. Were you appalled and wondered what being had suddenly overtaken the mind of your offspring? When you reprimanded the child for using such language, did the child state, "but you said that word last night?" How did you respond? Did you respond with "do what I say, not what I do. I'm an adult" or did you think of how important it was to show your child appropriate behaviors instead of stating what *should* be done while doing the opposite?

Leaders must lead by example. Leaders must model behaviors that they wish their teams to exhibit. Leaders who exhibit professionalism promote those behaviors. Those who exhibit gossiping, belittling, or cliquish behaviors can expect the same from their teams. These individuals cannot afford to be upset when those team members react in the same manner. While we can state what behaviors are acceptable, what we model is truly our character. Those watching us as leaders will not remember what we said, but what we did, how we responded, and what we chose to display especially when these responses do not coincide with our words. Although everyone may not listen, someone is always watching. Behaviors that we assume will not negatively impact who we are and what our teams think of us can cause us to lose merit and credibility when witnessed.

Human beings are very sensual creatures. What we see is what we experience. What we hear becomes our reality. Very few adults would allow a person to tell them the sky is green and the grass is purple or that a bear tweets like a bird and a bird barks like a dog. We would probably think that person has taken an illegal substance. We know what we see. We know what we hear. We know what that person said and what words they claim is truth, but our reality is in what we experience.

The same is true for how we present as leaders. People can remember what we said, but it does not and will not out weight or outshine how we act, interact, and react to situations. Our words can be beautifully soliloquized, but our actions are what will stand out in the minds of those who cross our paths. What will people remember when they think of the leader you are?

Build a legacy of leadership that reflects your past, your present, and your future hopes and dreams. Build in others what was built in you. Be a leader whose actions speak volumes. Be a leader who promotes the positive. Be a leader who acts as a leader. Let your actions, interactions, and reactions reflect who you are as a leader. Be one who upholds and uplifts. Be strong, be resilient, be caring, and be genuine. Be a leader whose legacy will long surpass your time here on Earth. Build a legacy of leadership.

Further Thought: What Can I Do?

1. What insights and lessons can you gain from past and present experiences?
2. What can you do to increase your leadership potential? Learning opportunities, degrees, networking, etc.?
3. What can you do to prepare for your next move?
4. What steps can you take to move from your current leadership style to your targeted leadership style?
5. What relationships can you build to ensure successful outcomes?
6. How can you prepare your team and associates for succession?
7. How can you show leadership, not in word alone, but in actions?

REFERENCES

Alton, Y., & Forbes Technological Council (2021). *Pandemic fuels global growth of entrepreneurship and startup frenzy.* Retrieved from https://www.forbes.com/sites/forbestechcouncil/2021/04/09/pandemic-fuels-global-growth-of-entrepreneurship-and-startup-frenzy/?sh=713765ac7308

Gallup (2022). *State of the global workplace: 2022 Report.* Retrieved from https://www.gallup.com/workplace/349484/state-of-the-global-workplace.aspx?utm_source=google&utm_medium=cpc&utm_campaign=gallup_access_branded&utm_term=&gclid=Cj0KCQjwhY-aBhCUARIsALNIC06aAtR_6yVEeYdZcqZD4dk9NC9SIEk6nIshIInJTCEqC47oerKxmwwaAv50EALw_wcB

Gallup (2015). *State of the American manager.* Retrieved from https://www.gallup.com/services/182138/state-american-manager.aspx?thank-you-report-form=1

Genos International (2021). What is emotional intelligence? Dr. Ben Palmer breaks it down to Marie El Daghl. Retrieved from https://www.genosinternational.com/emotional-intelligence-at-work-podcast/what-is-emotional-

intelligence-dr-ben-palmer-breaks-it-down-to-marie-
el-daghl/transcript-season-1-episode-0/

Haraida, B., & Blass, E. (2019). Recognising "true" leadership:
The theory of natural born leadership. *International Journal
of Business and Social Science*. Retrieved from http://ijbssnet.
com/journals/Vol_10_No_4_April_2019/1.pdf

Hess, A. J. (2020). *82% of college grads believe their bachelor's degrees
was a good investment – but most would make this one change.*
CNBC: Make It. Retrieved from https://www.cnbc.
com/2020/02/27/82percent-of-college-grads-believe-
their-degree-was-a-good-investment.html

King James Bible (2017). Cambridge University Press. (Original
work published 1769)

Kohlrieser, G. (2014). Resilient leadership: Navigating the
pressures of modern working life. Retrieved from
navigating-the-pressures-of-modern-working-life/

New Living Translation. (2015). New Living Translation.
(Original work published 1996)

Society for Human Resource Management (2020). Survey: 84
percent of U. S. workers blame bad managers for creating
unnecessary stress. Retrieved from https://www.shrm.
org/about-shrm/press-room/press-releases/pages/survey-
84-percent-of-us-workers-blame-bad-managers-for-
creating-unnecessary-stress-.aspx

TRImani Consulting, LLC. (2021). *Leveraging Your Leadership
Journey: Using Insights from the Past to Build a Legacy of
Success* [PowerPoint Slides].

University of California at Berkeley (2021). What's the difference between a supervisor and a manager? Retrieved from https://hr.berkeley.edu/node/3818

University of Washington (2021). *What can students do to improve their chances of finding employment after college.* Retrieved from https://www.washington.edu/doit/what-can-students-do-improve-their-chances-finding-employment-after-college

Wastrom, J. (2020). *Why leaders must listen, and not just hear.* Forbes Magazine. Retrieved from https://www.forbes.com/sites/johnnywarstrom/2020/06/16/why-leaders-must-listen-and-not-just-hear/?sh=466fcc35bcfc

Western Governor's University (2020). Leadership theories and styles. Retrieved from https://www.wgu.edu/blog/leadership-theories-styles2004.html

Woodward, I. C. (2017). *Leadership is a journey, not a destination.* Retrieved from INSEAD Blog https://knowledge.insead.edu/blog/insead-blog/leadership-is-a-journey-not-a-destination-7581